FINAL DRAFT

3

DRAFT

Teacher's Manual

Series Editor: **Jeanne Lambert**
The New School

Andrew Aquino-Cutcher
Harold Washington College at the City Colleges of Chicago
Wendy Asplin
University of Washington
David Bohlke
Jeanne Lambert
The New School

with

Monica F. Jacobe, The College of New Jersey
Alan S. Kennedy, Columbia University
Emily Ann Mathis, University of Oregon
Sara Stapleton, North Seattle College
Linda Van Doren, Emily Griffith Technical College
and
Jane Stanley March

CAMBRIDGE
UNIVERSITY PRESS

CAMBRIDGE
UNIVERSITY PRESS

32 Avenue of the Americas, New York NY 10013-2473, USA

Cambridge University Press is part of the University of Cambridge.

It furthers the University's mission by disseminating knowledge in the pursuit of education, learning and research at the highest international levels of excellence.

www.cambridge.org

Information on this title: www.cambridge.org/9781107495548

© Cambridge University Press 2016

First published 2016

Printed in Mexico by Editorial Impresora Apolo, S.A. de C.V.

A catalog record for this publication is available from the British Library.

ISBN 978-1-107-49549-4 Student's Book Level 3
ISBN 978-1-107-49550-0 Student's Book with Writing Skills Interactive Level 3
ISBN 978-1-107-49554-8 Teacher's Manual Level 3

Additional resources for this publication at www.cambridge.org/finaldraft

Art direction, book design, and photo research: emc design limited
Layout services: emc design limited

CONTENTS

INTRODUCTION

Final Draft *is a four-level academic writing series for high beginning / low intermediate- to high advanced-level students of North American English.* The series prepares students to write in a college or university setting by focusing on the topics, rhetorical modes, skills, vocabulary, and grammar necessary for students to develop their academic writing. Students are given the tools to master academic writing. First, they learn and practice foundational academic writing skills essential to writing paragraphs and essays. Then, following a process-based approach, students move through the writing process, from brainstorming with graphic organizers to organizing and developing their ideas with outlines, before completing the final draft of their unit assignment.

Final Draft *provides frequent and realistic writing models.* Each unit features writing models that reinforce the concept that writing is purposeful. The Writing in the Real World article engages students and introduces them to the topic, ideas, language, and elements of structure or rhetorical mode taught in the unit. The Student Model then demonstrates the conventions of the target structure and mode. This progression from authentic text to traditional academic writing helps students new to academic discourse first understand the purpose of communicating with a given mode before turning their attention to mastering the form.

Final Draft *focuses on key academic vocabulary.* Students need to encounter high-frequency academic vocabulary and learn how to use it naturally in preparation for college-level writing. The academic phrases and collocations in the series were selected based on the findings of research into the *Cambridge English Corpus*. Analysis of this multibillion-word collection of real-life English indicates the language that is most relevant for academic writing, with a focus here on longer lexical chunks. The academic vocabulary in the series is also corpus-informed, the majority of words coming from Averil Coxhead's Academic Word List (AWL) and the remaining items taken from Michael West's General Service List (GSL). AWL words are identified as such in the index of the Student's Book.

Vocabulary items are contextualized and recycled throughout the unit. Academic collocations or academic phrases are introduced and practiced in alternating units. The writing models recycle these words and phrases in academic contexts, and in the final section of each unit students are prompted to find places where they can use these vocabulary items naturally when writing their end-of-unit assignment.

The grammar presented in **Final Draft** *is corpus-informed.* Corpus research tells us the most common grammar mistakes for specific grammar points in academic writing. Students study the most common grammar mistakes drawn from the *Cambridge Learner Corpus*, a unique collection of over 50 million examples of nonnative speakers' writing. Students then work to repair them in editing activities. At the end of the unit, students are reminded to correct these mistakes as they write their assignment, which helps promote accuracy in their writing.

Final Draft *teaches students to understand and avoid plagiarism.* The series provides a robust presentation of techniques for understanding and avoiding plagiarism. Each unit includes an overview of a common plagiarism-related issue, along with a skill-building activity. This innovative approach is pedagogical, not punitive. Many ESL students struggle with a range of issues related to plagiarism. By including realistic examples and practical activities in each unit, *Final Draft* helps students avoid plagiarism and improve their academic writing.

Writing Skills Interactive *provides extra practice in key writing skills.* This online course, which can be purchased with *Final Draft*, provides graduated instruction and practice in key writing skills to help students build confidence and fluency. Each unit provides an animated presentation of the target writing skill, along with automatically graded practice activities. Each unit closes with a quiz so students can assess their progress.

Special Sections

YOUR TURN ACTIVITIES

Each unit includes a wide variety of regular writing practice activities, including Your Turn activities, which ask students to go beyond traditional practice to apply the skills, ideas, and language they have learned to their selected writing prompt. As a result, by the time they write their end-of-unit assignment, they are thoroughly prepared for the writing process because they have already practiced relevant skills and generated useful ideas and language to incorporate into their work. This makes the writing process less daunting than it would otherwise be.

Series Levels

Level	Description	CEFR Levels
Final Draft 1	Low Intermediate	A2
Final Draft 2	Intermediate	B1
Final Draft 3	High Intermediate	B2
Final Draft 4	Advanced	C1

Additional teacher resources for each level are available online at cambridge.org/finaldraft.

Final Draft 3

This book is designed for a semester-long writing course. There is enough material in the Student's Book for a course of 50 to 70 class hours. The number of class hours will vary, depending on how much of a unit is assigned outside of class and how much time a teacher decides to spend on specific elements in class. Because units are carefully designed to build toward the final writing activity, teachers are encouraged to work through each unit in chronological order. However, units can generally stand alone, so teachers can teach them in the order that best suits their needs.

Unit Overview and Teaching Suggestions

UNIT OPENER

Purpose

- To introduce the unit topic and academic discipline in an engaging way
- To elicit preliminary thinking about the unit theme and structure or rhetorical mode

Teaching Suggestion

Have students respond to the quote in writing by freewriting their ideas or by agreeing or disagreeing with the central message of the quote.

1 PREPARE YOUR IDEAS

In Section 1, students begin to explore the unit structure or rhetorical mode and choose their writing prompt for the unit.

Ⓐ Connect to Academic Writing

Purpose

- To introduce the unit structure or rhetorical mode in an accessible way
- To connect academic writing to students' lives and experience

Teaching Suggestion

To deepen the conversation, elicit additional examples from students of how the rhetorical mode connects to thinking they already do in their lives.

Ⓑ Reflect on the Topic

Purpose

- To show a writing prompt that elicits the rhetorical mode
- To introduce an appropriate graphic organizer for brainstorming and organizing ideas for the mode
- To choose a prompt for the unit writing assignment and begin generating ideas for the topic
- To engage students with the writing process early in the unit

Teaching Suggestion

Group students together who chose the same writing prompt and have them brainstorm ideas for the topic. Groups can then share their ideas with the class and receive immediate feedback.

2 EXPAND YOUR KNOWLEDGE

In Section 2, students learn academic vocabulary and read a real-world text that contains elements of the unit structure or rhetorical mode.

Ⓐ Academic Vocabulary

Purpose

- To introduce high-frequency academic words from the Academic Word List and the General Service List
- To focus on the meaning of the target vocabulary within a thematic context

Teaching Suggestion

Have students choose vocabulary words from the activity that they still have trouble understanding or contextualizing and write sentences using them. They can share their sentences in groups or with the class and receive immediate feedback.

Ⓑ Academic Collocations / Academic Phrases

Purpose

- To teach academic collocations and phrases that frequently occur in academic reading and writing
- To encourage the use of language chunks that will make student writing more natural and academic
- To tie academic vocabulary to the unit theme

Teaching Suggestion

Have students use the Internet to find more authentic examples of the collocations in sentences as a homework assignment. Students can then share their examples with the class or in groups.

Ⓒ Writing in the Real World

Purpose

- To provide authentic content, ideas, and language in a context related to the unit theme
- To introduce elements of the unit rhetorical mode in an authentic reading
- To recycle new academic vocabulary and collocations or phrases
- To introduce features of the unit structure or mode

Teaching Suggestion

After students have read and understood the text, assign a paragraph or section to small groups, and have students work together to explain the purpose of each sentence in the section. Sample student responses: *The first sentence <u>introduces</u> the topic, the second and third sentences <u>give background information</u> on the topic, etc.*

3 STUDY ACADEMIC WRITING

In Section 3, students read and analyze a student model of a traditional academic paragraph or essay. A detailed examination of elements of the unit structure or rhetorical mode follows.

Ⓐ Student Model

Purpose

- To provide an aspirational student model for the unit structure or rhetorical mode
- To deepen understanding of writing technique through real-time analysis
- To provide a context for writing skills that will be studied in Section 4
- To familiarize students with writing prompts that can be answered using the unit mode
- To recycle academic vocabulary and collocations or phrases
- To evaluate and generate more ideas on the unit theme
- To demonstrate the organization and development of ideas in traditional academic writing

Teaching Suggestion

In small groups, have students discuss their answers to the Analyze Writing Skills tasks. Then have each group present to the class on something they noticed that they found interesting or still have questions about. This offers an opportunity to deepen the discussion on writing technique.

Ⓑ Unit Structure or Rhetorical Mode

Purpose

- To deepen understanding of the unit structure or rhetorical mode
- To explain key elements of the unit structure or rhetorical mode
- To have students practice writing elements of a paragraph or essay

Teaching Suggestion

Following the activities in this section in chronological order will ensure that students have covered all the key features of the unit structure or rhetorical mode. However, if students need less work in some areas, you may want to skip those parts in class and assign the activities for homework.

In general, practice activities, including Your Turn activities, can be completed in class and immediate feedback can be given by peers or the instructor. Alternately, these sections can be assigned as homework and brought to class for review.

4 SHARPEN YOUR SKILLS

In Section 4, students review and practice key writing skills, specific applications of grammar for writing, and ways to avoid plagiarism.

A Writing Skill

Purpose

- To provide practice with discrete writing skills that students can apply to their unit writing assignments
- To deepen knowledge of rhetorical strategies

Teaching Suggestion

Collect writing samples from one or more of the Your Turn activities in this section. Reproduce several for the class – on the board, as handouts, on a screen – to use as an editing activity.

B Grammar for Writing

Purpose

- To present specific applications of grammar for academic writing
- To draw attention to the most common grammar mistakes made by students
- To promote grammatical accuracy in academic writing
- To improve students' editorial skills

Teaching Suggestion

After students complete the editing task at the end of the section, have students identify elements of the unit mode (e.g., language, structure) and parts of an academic paragraph (e.g., topic sentence, examples, other supporting details).

C Avoiding Plagiarism

Purpose

- To increase awareness of the issues surrounding plagiarism
- To build skills and strategies for avoiding plagiarism
- To provide regular practice of writing skills useful for avoiding plagiarism

Teaching Suggestion

Have one student read the student question in the Q & A aloud; all other students should listen with their books closed. Elicit possible responses from the class and then compare them to the professor's answer in the book.

5 WRITE YOUR PARAGRAPH OR ESSAY

In Section 5, students go through the steps of the writing process to a final draft of their unit writing assignment.

STEP 1: BRAINSTORM

Purpose

- To brainstorm, evaluate, and organize ideas for the student paragraph or essay

Teaching Suggestion

After students brainstorm their own ideas on paper, survey the class and list the top three to five ideas for each writing prompt on the board. Then have the students explain, evaluate, and rank the ideas.

STEP 2: MAKE AN OUTLINE

Purpose

- To help students organize their paragraphs or essays before writing

Teaching Suggestion

After students complete their outlines, have them work in pairs to explain how key ideas in their outlines connect to the overall topic or thesis of their paper. This process helps confirm that their ideas are directly relevant to the topic and allows students to consider their ideas more fully.

STEP 3: WRITE YOUR FIRST DRAFT

Purpose

- To give students the opportunity to use the language, skills, and ideas from the unit to answer their writing prompt

Teaching Suggestion

After students write their first drafts, have students work in pairs to give each other feedback before turning in their writing to you. Ask partners to underline sections they think are well written and circle any words, sentences, or phrases that are unclear. Students can then revise for clarity before submitting their first drafts.

STEP 4: WRITE YOUR FINAL DRAFT

Purpose

- To evaluate and implement instructor/peer feedback
- To improve self-editing skills
- To write a final draft

Teaching Suggestion

Have students mark – highlight, underline, circle, number, etc. – sentences or parts of their writing that they revised based on peer or instructor feedback. This ensures students will incorporate some corrective feedback.

Assessment Program

The final section of the Teacher's Manual consists of an assessment program for *Final Draft*. It includes the following for each unit:

- Vocabulary quiz
- Grammar quiz
- Avoiding Plagiarism quiz
- Bank of additional writing prompts

Quizzes may be used individually or in combination with one or more of the others, depending on teacher and student needs. They are photocopiable, with downloadable versions available at cambridge.org/finaldraft. The Assessment Answer Key includes:

- General rubrics for academic writing (paragraphs / essays)
- Unit answer keys for vocabulary, grammar, and avoiding plagiarism quizzes

① INTRODUCTION TO THE ESSAY

ENVIRONMENTAL STUDIES: GREEN LIVING

Page 13

Possible answers:

1 Consumers can save the planet because they can change the behaviors that are causing pollution and make the planet healthier.
2 People use too much gas and electricity and they throw away a lot of toxic things that pollute the environment, like plastics and electronics.
3 I could use less plastic and reuse and recycle more.

1 PREPARE YOUR IDEAS

ⓑ Reflect on the Topic page 14

 1.1 page 14

Answers will vary.

2 EXPAND YOUR KNOWLEDGE

ⓐ Academic Vocabulary page 16

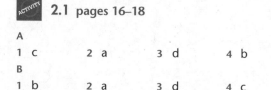 **2.1** pages 16–18

A
1 c   2 a   3 d   4 b
B
1 b   2 a   3 d   4 c

ⓑ Academic Collocations page 17

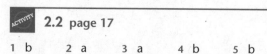 **2.2** page 17

1 b   2 a   3 a   4 b   5 b

ⓒ Writing in the Real World page 18
Possible answers: A life "unplugged" means that the person has a simple lifestyle that respects the environment. I think people want to live very simply because they like to be close to nature and natural things. They probably also care about the environment.

 2.3 page 19

1 A desire to go green, a rejection of consumerism, and economic necessity are the three main reasons people want to live in off-grid communities.
2 *Possible answer:* Off-grid living means that people live simply. Their lifestyle does not pollute the land as much and they have more time to spend enjoying nature and other people.
3 *Possible answer:* I would not like it. I like my phone too much and I would miss talking to people on social-networking sites.

 2.4 page 19

1 He has the reader visualize themselves living a simple lifestyle.
2 In the last sentence.
3 The purpose of paragraphs 2, 3, and 4 is to explain the reasons people choose a simple life and to convince the reader that this type of lifestyle is a good alternative for some people because it is good for the environment.

3 STUDY ACADEMIC WRITING

ⓐ Student Model page 20
Possible answers:

1 The writer will discuss how bike-share programs are good for cities and the people who live in them.
2 The writer might mention that a bike-share program makes people healthier and reduces traffic.

Analyze Writing Skills pages 20–21

1 Circled: b
2 Underlined: A bike-share program is good for cities and the people who live there because it is a convenient way to travel, it improves life in the city, and it makes people healthier.
3 Underlined: Commuters who travel to the city can ride around and go wherever they want … . In addition, bike stations are everywhere, so it is usually easy to find and park a bike.
4 Underlined: In addition,
   Circled: c
5 Circled: c
6 c

3.1 page 22

1 The essay is about bike-share programs and how they help cities and people.
2 *Possible answer:* The most convincing reason is its effect on people's health since many people get less exercise today and that is causing health problems in old and young people.
3 *Possible answer:* I'm not sure. I have never seen one. I think they are good for some people, but I wouldn't use it. I prefer to drive or take the bus.

 3.2 pages 22–23

I Introductory paragraph
  Thesis statement: <u>A bike-share program is good for cities and the people who live there because it is a convenient way to travel, it improves life in the city, and it makes people healthier.</u>
II <u>Easy to use</u>
  A Commuters – can ride and go everywhere
    1 Do not have to rely on bus/train schedules
    2 Car – too much traffic
  B Bike stations are everywhere
    1 <u>Easy to find and park a bike</u>
    2 One problem – supply
    3 App – to find bikes
III City more enjoyable and safer
  A <u>Fewer cars, less traffic and noise</u>
    1 Feel comfortable traveling
    2 Spend more time enjoying city
    3 Attract tourists
  B City feels less dangerous
    1 <u>Coming home from work – feel safer</u>
IV Positive effects on health
  A <u>Exercises whole body</u>
    1 I ride 5 miles a day
  B Good source of energy
    1 My experience – feel energetic
  C <u>Reduces stress</u>
V Concluding paragraph

The Essay in Academic Writing

 3.3 page 24

1 c   2 b   3 c

 3.4 page 25

Possible answers:
1 The author John Platt in "Going Off the Grid" asks the reader to visualize living simply. I think it is effective because it makes me feel personally connected to the topic.
2 The writer of the Student Model essay gives an interesting observation. This is effective because I am curious about where she lives and what she will say.

 3.5 page 26

1 The background information for the introductory paragraph for the professional author's essay explains the trend and why people choose off-grid living.
2 The background information for the introductory paragraph for the Student Model essay includes a personal story and some general information about bike shares.

 3.7 page 27

Professional author's essay:
The thesis statement is "For people who want to get away from today's consumerist society or help protect the environment, living off-grid can be an attractive option." It states the points, but not in the order that the author explains them.

Student Model essay:
The thesis statement is "A bike-share program is good for cities and the people who live there because it is a convenient way to travel, it improves life in the city, and it makes people healthier." It states the points in the order in which they appear.

3.8 page 28

1 b   2 a   3 a   4 a

3.10 page 29

First, a bike-share program is easy for people to use. Commuters who travel to the city can ride around and go wherever they want. They do not have to rely on the schedules of buses and trains. Driving a car is also difficult because of traffic. In addition, bike stations are everywhere, so it is usually easy to find and park a bike. One problem sometimes is that the supply of bikes is less than the demand for them. That was a problem in my city. However, we now have an app that tells where there are available bikes, so people do not have to spend time searching for one. Therefore, the bike-share program is more convenient than buses and other kinds of transportation.

 3.11 page 29

Possible answers:

1 Cities that have community gardens have better air quality.
2 Bikes save consumers a lot of money.

 3.13 page 30

Possible answers:

1 There could be more accidents with other bikes and cars.
2 There might not be bikes available when people need them.
3 Riding a bike can be dangerous in some areas of the city.

 3.14 page 30

Possible answer: Using a bike-share program is not always convenient or safe.

 3.15 page 30

Possible answers:

Body Paragraph 1 Topic Sentence: First, there could be more accidents with other bikes and cars.

Body Paragraph 2 Topic Sentence: Another drawback is that there might not be bikes available at bike lots when people need them.

Body Paragraph 3 Topic Sentence: Finally, riding a bike can be dangerous in some areas of the city.

 3.16 page 31

Possible answer:

First, there could be more accidents with bikes and cars. Riding a bike is a skill, so bikers need to practice before they use the bike lanes. They need to learn how to react when the streets are bumpy so that they do not run into people and cars. Car drivers need to learn to be aware of bike lanes and bikes so that they do not hit them. If drivers are not aware that there is a bike lane, they will not see the bikes. This happened to a friend of mine. He was riding his bike when a car suddenly went in front of him. He ran into the car and was in the hospital. Accidents are one drawback of bike-share programs.

 3.17 page 31

an opinion

 3.18 page 32

1 c   2 a

 3.19 page 32

Possible answer: Biking is a good way for people to be healthier, have more money, and feel less stress.

4 SHARPEN YOUR SKILLS

Ⓐ Writing Skill: Thesis Statements
page 33

 4.1 pages 33–34

1 b   2 b

Ⓑ Grammar for Writing: Infinitives page 35

 4.2 page 35

1 to protect   3 to heat   5 to enjoy
2 to create   4 to cost   6 to be

Avoiding Common Mistakes page 36

 4.3 page 36

Some people want ~~living~~ (to live) in very small houses because these homes use fewer natural resources. Because they are small, it costs less ~~for~~ (to) heat these homes. Also, they use less electricity than large houses because it costs much less per month ~~for~~ (to) supply electricity to a small house than to a large house. This is because small houses have fewer rooms, fewer electrical outlets, and less need for light fixtures than larger houses. Small houses use less water, too. Finally, they tend ~~to not~~ (not to) be on large lots. Therefore, they do not have large gardens that require ~~to water~~ (watering). The decision ~~to not~~ have a lot of space means that owners of small homes not only reduce energy consumption, but save valuable resources and money as well.

C Avoiding Plagiarism page 37

 4.4 page 38

Student B plagiarized.

 4.5 page 38

Answers will vary.

2 COMPARISON AND CONTRAST ESSAYS 1

EDUCATION: APPROACHES TO LEARNING

Page 15

1 Gardner meant that when people fail too many times, they sometimes cannot deal with the failure. They stop learning.

2 *Possible answer:* Some other reasons people stop learning include: an inability to pay for their education, no time to study, no support or help when classes get hard.

3 *Possible answer:* The most important reason that people stop learning is a bad experience at school. When students feel supported by instructors and other personnel, they are more likely to stay motivated and deal with difficulties.

---

 1 PREPARE YOUR IDEAS

B Reflect on the Topic page 44

1.1 page 44

Answers will vary.

2 EXPAND YOUR KNOWLEDGE

A Academic Vocabulary page 46

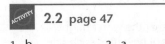 **2.1** page 46

A
1 c   2 d   3 a   4 b
B
1 d   2 a   3 c   4 b

B Academic Phrases page 47

2.2 page 47

1 b   2 a   3 c

C Writing in the Real World page 48

Possible answers:
Being smart means knowing a lot and being able to use one's knowledge in school and in real-world situations.
I think that some people are born smart, but everyone can get smart by working hard.

 2.3 page 49

1 The author is comparing how Asian and American students approach difficult problems, and how their culture and school systems set up different expectations about learning.

2 The difference in attitude lies in whether students are "born smart," or whether intelligence and academic success are a product of hard work and diligence.

3 *Answers will vary.*

1 The writer's use of the word "*however*" indicates that she is comparing the Japanese students to the American ones.

2 The writer is comparing how Japanese and American cultures perceive students' abilities to learn. The writer uses "on the other hand" to introduce differences.

3 In paragraph 10, the writer compares the scores of students who either believe that students are "born smart" or can "get smart." This comparison helps the writer prove that students' attitudes about their own ability can affect their test scores.

3 STUDY ACADEMIC WRITING

Ⓐ Student Model page 50

1 The essay prompt is asking the writer to compare two skills.
Circled words: *artistic*, *physical*, *experience*, *learning*

2 *Possible answer:* I think that the writer might compare them in terms of how hard each one was, how much money they cost, and what kind of equipment they used.

Analyze Writing Skills pages 50–51

1 Circled: learning to draw, play the saxophone

2 Underlined: I enjoyed learning to draw and play the saxophone, but they were very different experiences in terms of how I learned, how much I practiced, and how they made me feel.

3 Ordered as follows: a. 3 b. 1 c. 2

4 Underlined: In contrast, my experience learning to play the saxophone was different.

5 b

6 Underlined: In conclusion, learning to draw felt different from learning to play the saxophone in important ways. Even though learning the saxophone produced quicker results, I enjoyed the time and freedom I had when I was teaching myself how to draw.

1 The writer compared his experiences by how he learned, how much time he spent practicing, and how much freedom he felt learning each one.

2 He felt a lot more freedom drawing, and this made him want to practice more and gave him more satisfaction.

3 *Possible answer:* A teacher can help you learn the skill in an organized way, keep you motivated, and help you gain confidence in your ability.

I Introductory paragraph
Thesis statement: <u>I enjoyed learning to draw and play the saxophone, but they were different in terms of how I learned, how much I practiced, and how each one made me feel.</u>

II Learning to draw
A Learned on my own
1 Started by tracing anime characters
2 Able to draw them without looking
3 <u>Could draw from my imagination</u>
B Practiced whenever I could
1 Spent hours perfecting drawings
C <u>Felt a sense of freedom</u>
1 Experimented with new ideas and techniques
2 Free to express myself

III Learning to play the saxophone
A Took lessons at school
1 Had class once a week
2 <u>Relied on my teacher to learn</u>
B Practiced less, but improved faster
1 <u>Practiced one hour on Saturdays</u>
2 Learned new songs quickly
C <u>Felt less free</u>
1 Played songs teacher chose
2 A right way to play each song
3 <u>Expectation – sound like everyone else</u>

IV Concluding paragraph

B Comparison and Contrast Essays: Block Organization page 53

 3.3 page 54

1 c   2 a   3 c   4 b

 3.5 page 56

1 c   2 b   3 c

 3.6 page 57

Possible answers:

1 Learning another language is like learning a musical instrument because they both require time, <u>patience</u>, and <u>practice</u>.
2 Young learners and adults differ in <u>how they study</u>, <u>how they learn</u>, and <u>why they learn</u>.
3 Learning to read is like learning to drive a car because for both you must have patience, you <u>must practice</u>, and you <u>must learn skills</u>.

 3.7 page 58

1 D (are different in)
2 S (were similar in many ways)
3 D (fundamental differences)
4 B (have similarities, differ in one important way)
5 S (are similar)

 3.9 page 59

a 3   b 1   c 2

3.10 pages 60–61

Possible answers:

   In contrast, the schedule for college classes is different from high-school classes. <u>It varies a lot because there are many choices. Students can go to school during the day or at night. They can take many different classes, too.</u> Unlike homework for high school, homework for college <u>can be difficult. Usually it requires more time and some research. Some assignments are long and may not be due until the middle or end of a term.</u> Finally, compared to high-school teachers, college professors <u>are busier. If you want to discuss your work, you have to make an appointment. However, they care a lot, too, but you must try harder to get their help.</u>

 3.11 page 61

1 in two sentences
2 He realizes that drawing comes more naturally and gives him greater satisfaction. He learned that drawing is his true passion because it helps him express who he is as an individual.

4 SHARPEN YOUR SKILLS

A Writing Skill: Words and Phrases That Show Differences page 62

 4.1 pages 63–64

2 Unlike electronic textbooks, print textbooks take more time to buy. OR Unlike print textbooks, electronic textbooks are quick and easy to purchase and download.
3 Electronic textbooks are convenient. On the other hand, you have to have an electronic reader to use them.
4 While the number of students buying electronic textbooks is rising, some students say that they would rather read a print book.
5 Even though young learners and adult learners have striking differences, they both enjoy and learn from tasks that are interesting to them.
6 Though a good teacher is an important motivator for both young learners and adult learners, young learners rely on the help of a teacher much more.
7 Both young learners and adult learners learn through socializing and games. However, adult learners can also learn by themselves.
8 Young learners generally accept the information that the teacher gives them. In contrast, adult learners ask questions and may disagree with the teacher.

B Grammar for Writing: That Clauses page 64

 4.2 page 65

2 The author makes the claim that adults are more challenging to teach than children.
3 The author argues that the born-smart mindset hurts students.
4 Some students feel that online classes are not as difficult as traditional classes.
5 Researchers cannot draw the conclusion that online learning is as effective as traditional learning.

Avoiding Common Mistakes page 66

 4.3 page 66

             that
Most people assume success in life for many

means getting a college education. In fact, many

high school students spend their last few years
           they
assuming that will go to college and prepare for

it. Once in college, however, their optimistic belief
that
they can achieve their goal weakens. College is
                   that
hard. Current research shows students who are

successful have different mindsets from other, less

successful students. Low-performing students may
                are
have the impression that they failing because they

are not smart enough. Researchers have found that
this (impression)
is often not true. They claim intelligence has less

to do with success than people think. Successful

students are different from other less successful

students in their persistence, commitment, and

ability to deal with failure. They simply have the
               they
belief that can succeed through hard work.

C Avoiding Plagiarism page 67

 4.4 page 68

Chart

For Paraphrase 1, check:

• Use synonyms.
• Change parts of speech.
• Introduce ideas with: X reports/states/believes
  that … According to X …

For Paraphrase 2, check:

• Change parts of speech.
• Break up or change the order of ideas.

Questions:

1 Paraphrase 1 does not plagiarize.
2 *Possible answer:* Stigler claims that people who
  believe intelligence comes from talent rather
  than hard work do not understand the meaning
  of education.

---

③ COMPARISON AND CONTRAST ESSAYS 2

SOCIOLOGY: COMMUNITIES AND RELATIONSHIPS

Page 73

1 Alexie is referring to the conflict that people
  sometimes feel between how a group wants
  them to feel and act and how they personally
  want to feel and act.
2 *Possible answer:* When you are part of a
  community, you have to help others, obey the
  laws, and show respect to others.
3 *Possible answer:* I feel that it is better to be part
  of a community and be helpful to others.

1 PREPARE YOUR IDEAS

B Reflect on the Topic page 74

 1.1 page 74

Answers will vary.

2 EXPAND YOUR KNOWLEDGE

A Academic Vocabulary page 76

2.1 pages 76–77

A
1 d   2 c   3 a   4 b
B
1 b   2 c   3 a   4 d

B Academic Collocations page 77

2.2 page 77

1 a   2 a   3 b   4 a   5 a

C Writing in the Real World page 78

Possible answers:

Relationships in a community are of major
importance. People in a community can help each
other in difficult situations such as storms.

In difficult situations, both community and
infrastructure are important. Emergency services
can help people, but people in the community can
help one another.

2.3 page 79

1 The author's main idea is that human connections are an important factor in saving lives in any kind of disaster.
2 Community groups were able to help people when government agencies couldn't.
3 *Answers will vary.*

 2.4 page 79

1 The author compares two neighborhoods of Chicago, Englewood and Auburn Gresham.
2 The writer compares them in terms of demographics, death rate, and amount of social connection.
3 The comparison helps to show that connections between people can help people survive in difficult circumstances.

3 STUDY ACADEMIC WRITING

A Student Model page 80

Possible answers:

1 The essay will be about the ways that the writer's community has changed, such as the people who live there, the types of stores, and how these changes have made the community different.
2 I think that the writer might use the following words: *community, changed, recent years,* and *impact.*
3 The people, stores, traffic, and activities in communities can change. The writer could mention differences in the types of people, types of stores, how many people and stores, how much traffic, and types of entertainment.

Analyze Writing Skills pages 80–81

1 Underlined: Compared to before the light rail, Royalville today has a much stronger economy, more music and cultural events, and small differences in its ethnic diversity.
   Circled: before the light rail, today
2 Underlined: The economy is the most important difference between Royalville before the light rail and today.
   Circled: economy
3 both subjects
4 Underlined: Before the light rail, there were two clubs where local musicians played. AND Today there are a lot more lectures and classes at the library.

5 mostly similarities
   Circled: similarly (in the fourth sentence)
6 Underlined: For me, the neighborhood is definitely a better place today. I feel proud that my neighborhood has become desirable and that businesses are doing well. I believe communities have to adapt to be successful and to survive.

 3.1 page 82

1 The writer has seen her community change in terms of the economy, the music and cultural events, and the ethnic groups.
2 *Possible answer:* The most noticeable one is the change in the economy. The town has a lot more buildings, stores, and jobs.
3 *Possible answer:* I have seen some changes. There are more apartment buildings. There is a new electronic store and a department store. There is more traffic because there are more people.

 3.2 page 82

I Introductory paragraph
   Thesis statement: <u>Compared to before the light rail, Royalville today has a much stronger economy, more music and cultural events, and small differences in its ethnic diversity.</u>
II Economy
   A Before the light rail
      1 Not many businesses – difficult to find jobs
      2 People worked in the city nearby
      3 <u>Housing inexpensive</u>
      4 Unattractive and dirty
   B <u>Today</u>
      1 Economy improved
      2 New buildings and houses
      3 Cost of housing rose
      4 New types of businesses
      5 Easier to find jobs
III <u>Music and culture</u>
   A Before the light rail
      1 Music clubs
      2 Lectures and cultural programs at library
   B Today
      1 More places to hear music, programs at library
      2 Blues club
      3 <u>Galleries for artists</u>

IV Ethnic groups
  A Before the light rail
    1 Filipinos, Vietnamese, and East Africans
    2 <u>Small family restaurants</u>
    3 Ethnic food and clothing stores
  B After the light rail
    1 Same cultures, also Mexicans, Guatemalans, El Salvadorans
    2 Still small ethnic restaurants
    3 <u>Fewer ethnic food and clothing stores</u>
V Concluding paragraph

B Comparison and Contrast Essays: Point-by-Point Organization page 84

 3.3 page 84

1 d   2 a   3 c

 3.4 page 86

Possible answers:

1 Members' commitment is a significant difference because the soccer team feels a lot of responsibility and obligation to come and do their best, but members of a book club don't feel that way at all. The connection to the group is not as strong.

2 The cost is the difference that does not reveal anything. I think the writer feels that the money does not tell us about the people or relationships, or anything unique. I agree.

3 Achievement is the obvious difference. I think the writer does not include it because he thinks that the activities are so different that there is nothing to discuss about them. Plus, maybe he thinks he won't have anything worth saying by making such a comparison. I might use this difference if I wrote the essay.

4 I think the writer puts the ideas in order from least significant to most significant because the commitment to the group is the biggest difference.

 3.6 page 87

Item 3 is the clearest because it mentions both subjects, tells how it will compare them and that it will describe differences, and uses the language of comparison with words like *more* and *better*.

 3.7 page 88

Possible answers:

1 Compared to my neighborhood, Harmon has more people, more noise, and more places to eat and have fun.

2 Although my neighborhood and Greenwood are different because they have different types of people and different kinds of housing, they are similar because they both have nice parks.

 3.9 pages 89–91

Possible answer:

The opportunities to socialize and meet others are one difference between living in a city and a small town. In cities, there are typically many coffee shops, bars, and other places where you can meet new people. You can often meet people from different places and countries.

Another difference is the number of opportunities to have new experiences and learn new ideas. Cities have many cultural institutions such as museums and theaters. Universities and various organizations offer lectures, tours, and other opportunities to learn.

Finally, there are differences in opportunities to achieve success in a career. Since cities have many businesses and companies, you can more easily find a better job in your field. In cities, you have more of an opportunity to network and find people in your field and learn from them.

 3.10 page 90

1 Underlined point of comparison: Unlike a small town, it <u>is diverse</u>, <u>has a lot of ways to meet people</u>, and <u>offers more opportunities to meet and socialize with people who share similar interests</u>.

2 an opinion

4 SHARPEN YOUR SKILLS

A Writing Skill 1: Words and Phrases That Show Comparison page 91

 4.1 page 92

1 In high school, the students who join the Drama Club enjoy acting in theater productions. Similarly, students in music groups such as band and chorus like performing in school programs.

2 Recently, both knitting groups and sewing circles have become popular with young people.

3 The girls' swim team requires many hours of practice every week. Similarly, the swimmers' parents must spend many hours taking the girls to practice.

4 Members of both the Hiking Club and the Photography Club should have their own equipment.

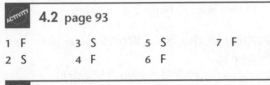 Writing Skill 2: Avoiding Sentence Fragments page 93

ACTIVITY 4.2 page 93

1 F	3 S	5 S	7 F
2 S	4 F	6 F	

ACTIVITY 4.3 page 94

One factor is the warning time. With earthquakes, communities do not have any warning. Therefore, ~~is~~ *it* is difficult to help others during the earthquake. People only have time to help themselves and react by doing the simple drills that they were ~~taught. Such~~ *taught, such* as getting under a desk or standing in a doorway. People in earthquake-prone areas should have emergency kits. ~~Because~~ *because* they do not know how long they might be without water or power. These items need to be stored in a convenient location so that people can grab them quickly. ~~For example,~~ *– for example,* under the bed. Unlike earthquakes, tornadoes can be tracked through satellite and radar technology. TV and radio stations provide tornado path reports. ~~Which~~ *, which* are updated regularly. People in those communities have time to get into a shelter below ground. They may also have time to drive away from the path of the tornado. In both cases, they may be able to help others in their community. ~~Since~~ *since* there is a little time before the disaster strikes.

Grammar for Writing: Identifying Relative Clauses page 94

ACTIVITY 4.4 page 95

2 Earthquakes that last for several minutes can be extremely damaging.

3 Many doctors who had special skills in emergency medicine helped out too.

4 Many months after a disaster, people may feel anxiety that they did not expect to feel.

5 Certain public buildings that the government identifies are used for temporary housing for survivors.

6 Communities whose residents have experienced a natural disaster before often recover more quickly after a disaster.

7 After a disaster, the water that people drink must be purified.

Avoiding Common Mistakes page 96

ACTIVITY 4.5 page 96

Neighborhood watch groups are one important difference. In my neighborhood we have a good neighborhood watch group that ~~it~~ has made the area a lot safer. Neighbors ~~which~~ *who* are concerned about crime work together. They watch the neighborhood for any unusual activity which ~~it~~ might be suspicious. Our neighborhood group has a block captain ~~which~~ *who* organizes meetings in the community. About once a year, the police ask an officer *who* watches the neighborhood to speak to the group about safety. Unlike my neighborhood, my friend's neighborhood does not have a neighborhood watch group. They have a lot of street crime. A few people put up signs *that* tell the criminals that they are being watched, but that is the only action they have taken. It is not very effective.

Avoiding Plagiarism page 97

 4.6 page 98

Checked: 1, 3, 4

 4.7 page 98

Checked: 2, 4

④ CAUSE AND EFFECT ESSAYS

TECHNOLOGY: SHARING ONLINE

Page 103

Possible answers:

1 I think it's natural because almost everybody loves sharing on social media. My family and I communicate a lot on social media and texting because we are far away from each other. It makes me so happy to see their pictures and messages.

2 I'm not sure about that, but I think that we want to feel that other people care for us. When people comment on our posts, it makes you feel special and connected to them.

3 I'm not sure about that because there are a lot of people who say really mean things on social media, too. There are people who bully others online too. This means that we are not understanding each other better.

1 PREPARE YOUR IDEAS

ⓑ Reflect on the Topic page 104

 1.1 page 104

Answers will vary.

2 EXPAND YOUR KNOWLEDGE

ⓐ Academic Vocabulary page 106

2.1 pages 106–107

1 b	3 a	5 a	7 b
2 a	4 a	6 b	8 a

Academic Phrases page 107

2.2 page 107

2 Underlined: teenagers have a place to share their ideas.
   Possible answer: As a result of online communities, people can easily stay in touch with friends in other countries.

3 Underlined: it promotes social skills
   Possible answer: The main impact of social media on young people is that they spend a great deal of time online and less time on face-to-face relationships.

ⓒ Writing in the Real World page 108

Possible answers:

TMI means too much information. It is used in response to people saying very personal things about themselves that make others embarrassed.

 2.3 page 109

1 The author doesn't believe that oversharing is a problem. He thinks that in the end it is good because it makes people feel better about themselves and helps them express themselves. It frees people from fearing what other people think of them or how other people judge them, and so they feel more secure.

2 The author mentions positive effects of oversharing such as the fact that it can make people happier and freer. It is making us freer because we feel less concerned about people who hate or people who disagree with us, and we feel safer because everyone knows us. He also mentions some negative effects. For example, he mentions that we risk that other people will use our personal information against us.

3 *Answers will vary.*

1 The writer's main idea is that oversharing makes us happier and freer and more secure in ourselves. He is stating an effect of oversharing.

2 The words in paragraph 1 that help us understand that the writer will focus on effects include *changed the way we work …*, *Because of this, we are redefining the lines …*, *making our lives more (transparent) …*, *Oversharing can have negative effects …*, and … *make us happier and freer.*

3 The cause is that Stephanie Klein is blogging and sharing her personal information online. The effect is that she has "a new sense of identity" and it has made her feel "more content offline." The purpose of the paragraph is to show the positive effects of sharing online.

3 STUDY ACADEMIC WRITING

A Student Model page 110

1 The essay topic is asking the writer to write about effects. The following words might be circled: *positive effects/benefits*, *negative effects/dangers*, *sharing information online.*

2 *Possible answer:* The writer might say that one positive effect of sharing is that people feel closer to other people because they can find out information more quickly and easily, and one negative impact might be that people say things that are hurtful and cause embarrassment.

Analyze Writing Skills pages 110–111

1 Boxed sentence: Through these sites, people are able to communicate with each other in an emergency, share information about events with everyone in the entire world, and collaborate with others to help make the world better.
The writer will focus on effects.

2 Underlined: to communicate with each other in an emergency, share information about events with everyone in the entire world, collaborate with others to help make the world better.
The points follow the same order in the paragraphs.

3 Circled: events, world, share

4 The primary effect of social media is

5 Underlined: The world is a lot closer because of online sharing, and that makes me feel hopeful about the future.

Possible answers:

1 I agree with the writer that social media is mostly positive and that it has helped make the world better.

2 Another example of a positive effect of online sharing is learning about good items to buy or good books to read.

3 I think there are more benefits to online sharing because even though there are dangers, people can avoid them. They can make their information private.

I Introductory paragraph
Thesis statement: <u>Through these sites, people are able to communicate with each other in an emergency, share information about events with everyone in the entire world, and collaborate with others to help make the world better.</u>

II <u>Ability to communicate in disasters</u>
  A Share information
    1 Can find out about rescue efforts and victims
    2 2014 landslide
      a Social media helped organize volunteers
      b <u>People used Twitter</u>

III Citizen journalists
  A Take photos and video of events
    1 <u>TV news programs and newspapers used them</u>
      a Recent protests
      b News programs used the information
  B Write about events
    1 Give their own perspectives
    2 <u>Help people become aware of the issues</u>

IV Become involved in organizations
  A Easier to volunteer
    1 Habitat for Humanity
  B <u>Crowdfund projects</u>
    1 PencilsofPromise
    2 Change.org
    3 Dosomething.org

V Concluding paragraph

B Cause and Effect Essays page 114

 3.3 page 115

Organization A

a   3

b   *Answers will vary.*

Organization B

a   3

b   *Answers will vary.*

 3.4 page 116

1   E (Smartphones are having a negative ⟨impact⟩ on our close relationships.)

2   C (The use of social media ⟨is causing⟩ problems in relationships.)

3   E (⟨If⟩ teenagers socialize mainly through social media, ⟨then⟩ they become less comfortable in making new friends face to face and they have fewer close friendships.)

4   C (There are three ⟨reasons⟩ that social media is more effective than other advertising for making brands successful.)

 3.6 page 117

2   **Topic Sentence 2:** Another reason that children bully is that their parents do not discipline them at home.

3   **Topic Sentence 3:** The primary reason that children bully is that they are unable to feel compassion for others.

3.8 page 118

Possible answers:

1   **Supporting sentence:** One positive effect of social media is that more young people know what is going on in the world.
   Example: Everyone has many different friends and interests. Friends share links to sites and information from all over the world about many different things, so it is easy to find out about events that they would never otherwise find out about. They also can promote their favorite causes and encourage their friends to help.

2   **Supporting sentence:** A second positive effect of using social media is that it enables people to feel more empathy for others.
   Example: People share celebrations and sad or difficult situations. For example, they share wedding photos and they share sad news about sickness and death. They often tell details, so people can feel empathetic and sympathize with them.

 3.10 pages 119–120

Possible answer:

One positive benefit of social media on traveling is that it allows tourists to stay in touch with their friends and family easily. Tourists can share their experiences as they occur, so family members can feel the excitement with them. Also, if tourists get lost or get into trouble, their family knows too and can help them. For example, if they are lost, their family can help them find the way and make them feel safe.

Finding recommendations from other travelers is another positive effect of using social media while traveling. There are many travel blogs. Travelers can use the blogs to find interesting museums, restaurants, and social events that not everyone knows about. There are also sites where people can rate and comment on their experiences. These sites are extremely helpful in making plans because travelers can become aware of places they should avoid, such as poor-quality restaurants and tourist attractions. Travelers make better choices because of social media.

A third impact of social media is that tourists are able to make or change travel plans with others quickly. When people want to plan a trip, they can easily share links and ideas and make decisions. If someone's travel plans change, he or she can tell everyone quickly and easily. Everyone can respond and the changes can be made online. Our lives are always changing but those changes are no longer problems because of social media.

 3.11 page 120

1   Yes

2   an opinion

3   *Possible answer:* Yes, because the writer repeats the positive effects of sharing online in a number of situations and because he gives his positive reaction to the sharing he has described.

4 SHARPEN YOUR SKILLS

A Writing Skill 1: Phrases That Show Cause and Effect page 121

 4.1 pages 121–122

2   due to

3   Because of

4   For this reason,

5   As a result of

4.2 page 122

Answers will vary.

B Writing Skill 2: Parallel Structure
page 123

 4.3 page 123

2 Local businesswomen use Twitter to support
   each other, get knowledge from others, and
   ~~growth of~~ *grow* their business.

3 For political protests, social-networking sites
   are a quick way to spread information, move
   people, and ~~for the organization of~~ *organize* events.

4 Teachers use social media for teaching,
   communicating with students, and ~~interact~~ *interacting*
   with other teachers.

5 Teens report that social networking makes them
   feel less shy, more outgoing, and ~~have~~ more
   ~~confidence~~ *confident*.

6 Most children use digital devices easily,
   confidently, and ~~they are enthusiastic~~ *enthusiastically*.

 4.4 page 124

Answers will vary.

C Writing Skill 3: Paragraph Unity
page 124

 4.5 page 124

Another serious effect of online bullying is
that it can affect students' studies and academic
performance. When students are bullied online,
they may not pay attention in class. They also
often stop participating in class, or taking part
in class discussion. They worry that if they talk in
class, they may be bullied more. ~~Teachers should
stop this.~~ Next, bullied students may start to
neglect their schoolwork. As a result, their grades
start to drop. ~~Colleges are not interested in people
with bad grades.~~ Many bullied students begin to
skip classes because they feel uncomfortable at
school. Some of these students finally quit school
altogether and never graduate. ~~Children who bully
usually do not have loving parents.~~

D Grammar for Writing: Real Conditionals
page 125

 4.6 page 126

Possible answers:

2 If/When people start a Twitter feed about an
   important environmental issue, such as clean
   air, followers spread the word to promote
   positive change.

3 If/When people share political messages about
   an event with others through social networks,
   there is more news coverage.

4 When schools offer programs about bullying,
   fewer children are bullied.

5 If a child feels no empathy for others, the child
   will probably become a bully.

Avoiding Common Grammar Mistakes
page 127

 4.7 page 127

Many problems can result from sharing the
wrong information on social media sites. First, if
someone ~~will share~~ *shares* personal information, such as a
cell phone number or an email address, that person
may be a victim of cybercrime. Many teens share
their email addresses online and do not realize the
danger. If a cybercriminal ~~get~~ *gets* access to someone's
personal site, they can use that information for
identity theft or fraud. Another problem that some
social media users can face is posting photos that
are later embarrassing. For example, a college
student might post a photo from a party at spring
break. Later, if she ~~will apply~~ *applies* for a job the employer
may see the photo and decide not to hire her.
Furthermore, when someone posts something on
the web, it ~~do~~ *does* not disappear. Users should always
remember that fact, and be careful in what they
post. The third problem with sharing inappropriate
information online relates to work. If an employee
~~will make~~ *makes* rude comments about a boss, a co-worker,
or a client online, they could lose their job. There
can also be problems~~,~~ if an employee shares
company secrets.

E Avoiding Plagiarism page 128

 4.8 pages 130–131

2 Nixon says that adolescents who bullied others also had other negative behaviors (149).
OR
Adolescents who bullied others also had other negative behaviors (Nixon 149).

3 Zuckerberg says, "Tech can fill our lives with meaning, rather than fear" (50).

 4.9 page 131

Nixon, Charisse L. "Current Perspectives: The Impact of Cyberbullying on Adolescent Health." *Adolescent Health, Medicine & Therapeutics* 123.1 (2014): 143–158. Web. 28 Feb. 2015.

Weed, Julie. "Temptation to Share Online Can Come Back to Haunt Teens." *SeattleTimes.com*. 10 Mar. 2012. Web. 12 Feb. 2013.

Zuckerberg, Randi. *Dot Complicated: Untangling Our Wired Lives.* New York: Harper, 2013. Print.

 **5 SUMMARY ESSAYS**

HEALTH: BALANCED LIFESTYLES

Page 137

Possible answers:

1 I think that "having a life" means that people live a good life and enjoy their family and friends and that people aren't focusing just on work and career.

2 I that she means that people think that their career is "having a life," but having a life means to enjoy family and friends. It doesn't mean working at your job.

3 Maybe she says this because she feels that she has confused the two in her life or that she realizes how important it is not to confuse them.

1 PREPARE YOUR IDEAS

B Reflect on the Topic page 138

 1.1 page 138

Possible answer:
The article is about why a tax on unhealthy foods would help Americans and why Americans might decide a tax is necessary.

2 EXPAND YOUR KNOWLEDGE

A Academic Vocabulary page 140

 2.1 page 140

A
1 c   2 a   3 d   4 b
B
1 b   2 a   3 d   4 c

B Academic Collocations page 141

2.2 page 141

1 b   2 b   3 a   4 a   5 a

C Writing in the Real World page 142

Possible answers:
I think that "mindful eating" means being careful of the kinds of foods you eat. If you are thinking about what you eating, you may be more careful in the kinds of foods you eat.

 2.3 page 143

1 "Mindful eating" means using your senses as you eat, eating more slowly, and giving more thought to your food as you are eating.

2 "Mindless eating" is causing the obesity epidemic. Studies show that when we are not thinking about what we are eating, we eat more.

3 *Possible answer:* I think I'm mostly a mindless eater because I eat quickly and sometimes don't feel like I have time to really enjoy my food.

2.4 page 143

1 The paragraph briefly explains an experiment by Brian Wansink. He gave people at the movies different-sized buckets of popcorn, and he found those with larger buckets ate more.

2 The writer includes the experiment because it illustrates that if we do not eat consciously, we eat more.

3 STUDY ACADEMIC WRITING

A Student Model page 144

Possible answers:

1 The article is about the benefits of a tax on foods that are high in fat and sugar.
2 The author uses the example of taxes on cigarettes, which resulted in a decrease in consumption. She also mentions the high cost of health care for the obese.

 3.1 page 146

1 d   2 a   3 b   4 c

Analyze Writing Skills pages 146–147

1 Circled: a, b, c, d
2 Underlined points:
   - She starts by saying that this tax would be effective because it has worked for other unhealthy habits.
   - The author mentions that Americans might not accept the tax because they do not like taxes, and they do not like the government to tell them what to do.
   - The author also argues that even though Americans dislike taxes, they would vote for the tax if they realized that health-care costs were high because of obesity.

3 a

 3.2 page 147

1 The purpose of the essay is to explain the author's ideas in the article "Should We Tax Unhealthy Foods?"
2 The student writer includes the following points:
   - It has worked for other bad habits.
   - Americans may not like it, but they might vote for it if they realized obesity causes higher health-care costs.
3 No, he doesn't.

 3.3 pages 147–148

I Introductory paragraph
   Main Idea of the Article: <u>In "A Tax on Unhealthy Foods," Michelle Embrich claims that the growing number of obese Americans is causing a serious health crisis in the United States and that a fat tax can help solve the issue.</u>

II Several reasons
   A Has worked for other unhealthy habits
      1 <u>Example – smoking</u>
         a Higher prices, fewer smokers
      2 <u>Research from Archives of Internal Medicine</u>
   B <u>Tax would not be acceptable</u>
      1 Americans do not like government to interfere
         a Unsuccessful attempt to ban sodas in NYC
      2 <u>National survey</u>
   C Americans might agree if they had to pay higher health-care costs
      1 <u>Healthcare expected to double</u>
      2 They would ask government to do something

B Summary Essays page 148

 3.4 page 149

1 shorter than
2 student writer's words
3 does not include

 3.5 page 150

In <u>"Is There a Link Between Music and Happiness?," Molly Edmonds</u> claims that <u>music makes people happy by chemically changing the brain. Music is an important part of many people's lives. While many people say that it has a positive effect on them, there has not been research to support their claims until now.</u>

 3.7 page 152

1 a   3 c   5 c   7 b
2 b   4 b   6 d   8 e

3.8 page 152

1 Item 1 is not a main idea because it does not include that it helps people eat less.
2 Item 2 is the best main idea because it states the effects of mindful eating.
3 Item 3 is not the main idea because it explains the term "mindful eating," but it does not state the effects that the author describes.

4 SHARPEN YOUR SKILLS

A Writing Skill: Purpose, Tone and Audience page 154

 4.1 page 155

Possible answers:

2 Researchers at the Mayo Clinic found that laughter can help you relieve stress and pain.
3 A recent study at Loma Linda University showed that watching funny movies is beneficial for people's memory.
4 Laughter can also help our learning ability because it exercises the brain.
5 I think that laughing while you do yoga is inappropriate because yoga should be serious.

B Grammar for Writing page 156

 4.2 pages 156–157

2 Steven Taylor describes the importance of work in primitive societies.
3 Taylor argues that there is too much emphasis on working.
4 Current research found that working too much causes depression.
5 The author said that there is a link between poor health and working too much.

Avoiding Common Mistakes page 157

 4.3 page 157

Possible answers:

In "Four-Legged Support," Samantha Joel argues _{that}^ there are health advantages in owning a pet. She ~~describes~~ explains that pet owners are less lonely, depressed, and stressed after getting a pet. The owners said _{that}^ they feel these benefits even when they had close relationships with other people. Joel goes on to say that pets are similar to friends because they can both make people feel better socially. In fact, one study ~~said~~ found that pets can help people handle rejection. This study also ~~presented~~ showed that owning a pet really can improve people's well-being.

C Avoiding Plagiarism page 158

 4.4 page 159

Check: 2, 3, 5

6 SUMMARY–RESPONSE ESSAYS

BEHAVIORAL SCIENCE: LANGUAGE AND CULTURE

Page 163

Possible answers:

1 Language is a window to the world because through it we see the world. Each language allows us to view the world a bit differently.
2 Learning a language has made me more aware of different perspectives of the world. It makes me more curious of other ways of living and helps me appreciate them.
3 Learning a language is necessary in this world because of globalization. Countries and cultures are linked together. More businesses are multinational, so it becomes necessary to communicate with other cultures.

1 PREPARE YOUR IDEAS

B Reflect on the Topic page 164

1.1 page 164

questions the author, thinks of personal examples, connects to class readings

2 EXPAND YOUR KNOWLEDGE

A Academic Vocabulary page 166

2.1 page 166

A
1 b   2 d   3 a   4 c
B
1 c   2 a   3 b   4 d

B **Using Academic Phrases** page 167

 2.2 page 167

1 For this reason,
2 the fact that
3 in part

C **Writing in the Real World** page 168

Possible answer: I think that people who are bilingual are smarter and are more interesting because they can offer more different points of view about many topics.

2.3 page 169

1 Bilingualism helps the brain because it helps people multitask better, it helps people prioritize information better, and it helps ward off symptoms of Alzheimer's.
2 *Possible answer:* Schools are eliminating bilingual programs because of political ideas. Some believe that bilingual education favors immigrant families.
3 The author doesn't think it's right that bilingualism is not popular. She thinks that bilingualism is important for the education of immigrant children in the United States.

 2.4 page 169

1 The author is explaining the ideas of others. She is summarizing them.
2 She is explaining the ideas of others.
3 The purpose is to give the author's argument about bilingual education. She uses the findings about bilingual education to support her argument that bilingual education should be more of a priority.

3 STUDY ACADEMIC WRITING

A **Student Model** page 170

1 The letter to the editor is about immigrants to the United States and why they are important to this culture and should not be pressured to assimilate and lose their native culture and language.
2 The author uses historical facts, research, statistics, and examples.

 3.1 page 172

A
1 a, b   2 a   3 b   4 a, b
B
1 The writer agrees with Banks that immigrants should keep their cultural identity.
2 The writer disagrees with Banks's belief that assimilation is always negative.

Analyze Writing Skills pages 172–174

1 a, b, c, d
2 b
3 a
4 b, d
5 To explain confusion that the student writer had about the argument in the letter to the editor

 3.2 page 174

1 According to the student writer, the author's main idea is that immigrants should not have to assimilate and "shed one's culture" in order to be successful in America.
2 According to the student writer, Banks makes the following three points:
   • The pressure to assimilate is poor advice.
   • The pressure to assimilate has negative effects on people.
   • People and biculturalism are important to this country, and we should respect them.
3 The student writer thinks that Banks should not have focused on the negative because his own experience has been positive: he was able to assimilate and keep his original culture. He also cites research by Francois Grosjean that supports his beliefs. Banks might be swayed by the arguments, but I think she would say that not everyone has such positive experiences. Some people struggle with their identity.

 3.3 pages 174–175

1 Introductory paragraph
Main Idea of the Article: In her letter to the editor in the *Brownsville Times*, Dr. Carla Banks, a history professor at Two Peaks College, argues that immigrants should not have to assimilate and "shed one's culture" in order to be successful in America.
Student Writer's Thesis:
Although I agree with Dr. Banks that immigrants should not lose their cultures, I do not agree that assimilation to a new culture always has negative effects. Immigrants can enjoy the many advantages of living in two cultures.

Body Paragraph 1 Summary

II Immigrants – should not have to assimilate

   A Pressure to assimilate – against U.S. history and poor advice

      1 People need to understand different cultures in global world

      2 Keeping cultures and languages keeps the country competitive

   B <u>Pressure to blend in – negative effects</u>

      1 Ex: daughter's friend – torn between two cultures

      2 Ex: friend – lost culture

   C <u>Biculturalism – important, should respect</u>

Body Paragraph 2 Response

III <u>Not my experience</u>

   A People cannot keep one's culture – disagree

      1 They can be bilingual

      2 Ex: my siblings and I

   B Author emphasizes assimilation's negative effects – disagree

      1 <u>Grosjean – social advantages</u>

      2 Banks's friend – not assimilated yet

      3 Grosjean – bilinguals more creative, flexible, successful

         a Banks's friend

Body Paragraph 3 Response

IV <u>One confusion – definition of assimilation</u>

   A Two definitions of assimilation

      1 Makes argument weaker

V Concluding paragraph

B **Summary–Response Essay** page 176

 3.4 page 176

Chart

1 First mention of the author's name: introductory paragraph

2 Your thesis: introductory paragraph

3 The main idea of the original article: introductory paragraph

4 The title of the article: introductory paragraph

5 A summary of the author's points: summary paragraph

6 Your personal experience, facts, and knowledge from other sources to support your responses: response paragraph

7 Your personal ideas, opinions, and reactions related to the writer's ideas: response paragraph

 3.5 page 178

Missing: d, e

 3.6 page 178

Possible answers:

   In his article "Why Culture Matters," Richard McCoy, a social worker for the California Department of Social Services, argues that maintaining cultural traditions is important for the mental health of immigrant children.

               OR

   According to Richard McCoy, a social worker for the California Department of Social Services, in "Why Culture Matters," maintaining cultural traditions is important for the mental health of immigrant children.

 3.8 page 180

1 d   2 b   3 a   4 c

 3.10 page 181

Answers will vary.

 3.11 page 182

Answer will vary.

4 SHARPEN YOUR SKILLS

A **Writing Skill 1: Coherence 1**
   page 184

 4.1 page 185

Answers will vary.

B **Writing Skill 2: Coherence 2**
   page 185

4.2 page 186

Possible answers:

1 The author describes a school that wanted the immigrant students to feel welcome. The school gave these students opportunities to share their cultures and countries.

2 Every spring, all of the international students organized a special cultural festival. These students spent a lot of time preparing for it.

3 The authors point out that the success of the program was partly due to the support of the faculty. They go on to say that its success was also due to students' enthusiasm and cooperation.

4 In my opinion, this kind of program is a valuable experience for everyone because it allows all students to socialize naturally. Also, it helps them to create new friendships.

C Grammar for Writing Skill: Passive Voice page 187

 4.3 page 188

1 A bill to fund bilingual education was approved by the Senate.

2 129 languages are spoken by immigrant students in the Seattle Public Schools.

3 Important benefits of being bilingual have been discovered.

4 The benefits of bilingual education have been debated for years.

5 The importance of bilingual education is recognized.

Avoid Common Mistakes page 188

 4.4 page 189

The article states that multinational corporations often have communication problems because of the different languages that ~~is~~ *are* spoken by their partners or clients. The author's solution is to hire multilingual employees who can communicate in those languages. However, it can be difficult to find qualified multilingual workers. Even when a qualified worker who speaks the languages ~~are~~ *is* found, it is not always practical to hire the person.

Corporations must decide which languages are mostly ~~been~~ *being* used and hire people who speak those languages. Another solution could be to hire translators through a translation company. These translators can ~~be translated~~ *translate* documents, phone calls or meetings, although they may work for several places at the same time. But can the company trust these translators? One solution is translation software, which is ~~been~~ *being* developed to translate conversations. Unfortunately, at this time idioms and slang are ~~being caused~~ *causing* inaccurate translations, so it is not a reliable solution. Further advances in technology will undoubtedly solve this problem.

D Avoid Plagiarism page 190

 4.5 page 191

Quote:
"They must insist on use of the native language in the only setting they can control: the home."

Paraphrase:
Schools = less bilingual ed. Due to political beliefs because it is mostly immigrants. So parents should speak native language.

Ayşe's own ideas:
I agree. My cousins don't speak our native language well. Their parents always try to speak English in the house.

 4.6 page 191

Answers will vary.

 ARGUMENTATIVE ESSAYS 1

ECONOMICS: DEMOGRAPHICS AND THE ECONOMY

Page 197

Possible answers:

1 When Carter says the United States is a "nation of differences," I think he means that the country has people who have different beliefs, lifestyles, cultures, and languages. People often disagree on how to govern and which laws to enact, so there is always a lot of discussion and disagreement.

2 I think he says these differences are the "source of our strength" because he feels that having people from many different backgrounds and cultures is a great advantage for the United States. I agree. For example, people from all over the world come here to work and share their ideas and knowledge. This helps the economy and makes the country stronger.

1 PREPARE YOUR IDEAS

B Reflect on the Topic page 198

1.1 page 198

Answers will vary.

2 EXPAND YOUR KNOWLEDGE

A Academic Vocabulary page 200

2.1 pages 200–201

1 b	3 b	5 b	7 b
2 a	4 a	6 a	8 b

B Academic Collocations page 201

2.2 page 201

1 a   2 b   3 a   4 a   5 a

C Writing in the Real World page 202
Possible answers: By diversity, I think the author means people from many different backgrounds and cultures. In my opinion, the writer will argue that having people from different backgrounds and cultures makes the economy stronger because they bring new ideas.

2.3 page 203

1 The economists studied the link between the economy and culture around the world from preindustrial times to the modern era. They found that countries with more diverse cultures developed more quickly.
2 *Possible answer:* Two other possible causes were:
   • Western values such as individual effect, freedom, and the spirit of enterprise
   • geography, with the West having better climate, more natural resources, and less disease
3 *Answers will vary.*

2.4 page 203

Possible answers:
1 I think the author includes an opposing argument because this helps the reader understand some of the debates about the topic. It makes me think that he knows a lot about the topic.
2 In paragraph 2, the statistics prove that the West grew more quickly than other areas. The authors want to argue that this growth occurred because the West was not geographically isolated and was open to other people. This openness affected the West's culture and economy.
3 This paragraph talks about other theories or reasons why the West evolved so quickly. It is interesting and helps me understand the topic better and judge the argument by Ashraf and Galor.

3 STUDY ACADEMIC WRITING

A Student Model page 204
1 The writer will argue whether tech companies should hire more women.
2 She will argue that more women should be in tech jobs.

Analyze Writing Skills pages 204–205
1 Underlined: Women have 52 percent of professional jobs in the United States (Warner), but they have only about 12 percent of tech jobs at technology "start-ups" (Gilpin).
   Circled: statistic
2 Underlined: they would be more innovative and more competitive, and society would be much stronger.
3 fact, statistic, example
4 two
   Underlined: According to a study by the *Harvard Business Review* (Zenger and Folkman), women were given higher ratings in their leadership abilities … . Also, since there are not many women in technology, women do not feel comfortable and they work harder.
5 two
   Circled: First, Second

3.1 page 206

1 The purpose of the essay is to explain why there should be more women in tech jobs.

2 *Possible answer:* I think the last argument is strongest because the explanation of the benefits to women and to society is really convincing. Women and families will live better lives. The reasons are logical and make sense.

3 *Possible answer:* I agree with the writer that more women should be in technology, but I think that many women do not want to do that kind of job because it doesn't seem interesting.

 3.2 pages 206–207

I Introductory paragraph

Thesis statement: <u>In fact, companies should hire more women in technology because they would be more innovative and more competitive, and society would be much stronger.</u>

II <u>Increase their innovation</u>
  A Give new perspectives on ideas
    1 Will challenge men's ideas
  B <u>Help design products for women</u>
    1 Women – 85% of consumer purchases
    2 Avoid wrong decisions

III Help companies be more successful
  A <u>Higher ratings in leadership abilities</u>
    1 Better at leading and achieving
    2 Ex: Sandberg and Mayer
  B Women work harder – less comfortable
    1 <u>Men may not work as hard</u>

IV Society will benefit
  A Jobs will help women take care of their families
    1 Help single mothers
    2 Help mothers who support their families
  B <u>Women can be role models for young girls</u>
    1 They can encourage girls to study for jobs in technology

V Concluding paragraph

B Argumentative Essays page 207

 3.3 page 209

Possible answers:

1 F (This is a fact because it gives a statistic that can be measured.)

2 A (This is an argument because it explains the writer's view on why there are more women who are teachers and nurses. It is not a fact. Not everyone will agree.)

3 A (This is an argument because it explains the writer's view and not everyone will agree. It isn't a fact.)

4 F (This is a fact because it gives a statistic that can be proven.)

 3.4 page 210

Possible answers:

1 O (This is an opinion because it does not give reasons why gender does not matter in the workplace.)

2 O (This is an opinion because it does not give reasons why companies should have parental leave laws.)

3 A (This is an argument because it gives reasons why immigrants help the economy, reasons that can be argued.)

4 A (This is an argument because it gives effects that countries with a high cost of education might suffer from, effects that can be argued.)

 3.5 page 210

Possible answers:

1 In my opinion, women with young children should be able to have a job outside the home because women can help provide money for the family and all people should be able to work.

2 The Olympic Games are good for creating goodwill in the world because they offer a chance for us to appreciate each other's accomplishments and they are a way to learn about other cultures through the stories of the athletes.

 3.7 page 211

1 introductory paragraph, concluding paragraph

2 as a hook, to prove a reason in a body paragraph

3 body paragraphs

4 concluding paragraph

 3.8 page 212

Possible answers:

1 The statistic is surprising and it makes me interested in the topic.

2 The writer helps me understand the issue by telling me what people on both sides of the issue think. She starts out by giving the opposing side ("Some people believe …" and "They feel …"). Then she presents a summary of her argument.

Possible answers:

Writing Prompt 1

1 S (The point of view is clear. It includes the key words *high-paying job*, *necessary*, and *happy life*. The reasons are clearly stated and each one can be argued by evidence.)

2 S (The point of view is clear. It includes the key words *high-paying job*, *necessary*, and *happy life*. The reasons are clearly stated and each one can be argued by evidence.)

3 W (The point of view is not clear. It is missing key words from the prompt. It seems to be too narrowly focused on one reason. It is not clear how the writer will support the reason.)

Writing Prompt 2

1 W (The point of view is not clear and does not contain *should*. It does not include key words from the prompt so it does not really answer the prompt.)

2 S (It has a clear point of view and contains *should*. It contains key words such as *Internet*, *be controlled*, and *governments*. The reasons are clearly stated and can be argued by evidence.)

3 S (It has a clear point of view and contains *should*. It contains key words such as *Internet*, *be controlled*, and *governments*. The reasons are clearly stated and can be argued by evidence.)

 3.11 page 214

Possible answers:

1 The writer might discuss other factors that are motivating, such as choosing a job based on what they love doing, choosing a job that is close to home, or choosing a job that is part of the family business.

2 The writer will discuss ways to show respect for each other's customs and values – for example, honest discussions about customs and values so that both sides understand them and their importance; learning about and sharing in holidays and celebrations; mutual creation of guidelines to follow for disagreements and conflicts.

- In a global survey on jobs by Gallup (qtd. in Gallo), over 80 percent (statistic) of people in the world did not care about their jobs.

- In my family, three of my uncles work in construction. (personal experience) They all complain about their job, but they have very good salaries, so they go to work every day. (example)

- If people want to work, they have to take the jobs that are available. (fact)

 3.13 page 216

1 a   2 b

 3.15 page 217

Possible answers:

1 The writer restates her argument in the first sentence. It basically repeats the ideas in the thesis statement in the first paragraph, in a shortened form.

2 The writer basically repeats the thesis statement, which points out that if tech companies hire more women, the companies, women, and society will benefit. The statement is convincing because the writer has provided support for each point in the body paragraphs of the essay.

3 The writer ends the essay with a call to action that is personal – what the writer will do herself. As a result, it is memorable.

4 The writer persuaded me to agree with her point of view. Her essay provided facts and examples that gave me a deeper understanding of the benefits and importance of tech companies hiring more women.

4 SHARPEN YOUR SKILLS

A Writing Skill 1: Avoiding Run-ons and Comma Splices page 218

 4.1 page 219

1 RO (*Possible answers:* Jimmy Carter said the U.S. is a nation of differences, and those differences are the source of our strength. OR Jimmy Carter said the U.S. is a nation of differences. Those differences are the source of our strength. OR Jimmy Carter said the U.S. is a nation of differences; those differences are the source of our strength.)

2 CS (*Possible answers:* The Internet connects people like never before, and this has created a global culture and economy. OR The Internet connects people like never before. This has created a global culture and economy. OR The Internet connects people like never before; this has created a global culture and economy.)

3 RO (*Possible answers:* A job is not just about paying the rent, and it can also increase a person's self-respect. OR A job is not just about paying the rent. It can also increase a person's self-respect. OR A job is not just about paying the rent; it can also increase a person's self-respect.)

4 RO (*Possible answers:* There is a perception that women are not good at computer programming, and many technology companies have very few women. OR There is a perception that women are not good at computer programming. Many technology companies have very few women. OR There is a perception that women are not good at computer programming; many technology companies have very few women.)

5 CS (*Possible answers:* Some people think welcoming people from different countries is bad for the economy, and others feel greater diversity is an advantage. OR Some people think welcoming people from different countries is bad for the economy. Others feel greater diversity is an advantage. OR Some people think welcoming people from different countries is bad for the economy; others feel greater diversity is an advantage.)

6 CS (*Possible answers:* A diverse workforce offers more skills and points of view, and this helps companies work better with different cultures in their markets. OR A diverse workforce offers more skills and points of view. This helps companies work better with different cultures in their markets. OR A diverse workforce offers more skills and points of view; this helps companies work better with different cultures in their markets.)

Ⓑ Grammar for Writing: Reduced Relative Clauses page 220

 4.2 page 221

2 New York City, known as the Big Apple, is one of the most diverse cities in the United States.

3 When you walk down the streets of New York City, you can hear people speaking many different languages.

4 In Toronto, a multicultural city, people speak over 140 languages.

5 Immigrants to Canada have skills needed for a strong economy.

6 Toronto has a strong network of community groups helping immigrants adjust to the city.

7 In both cities motivated immigrants can find the resources to create good lives.

Avoiding Common Grammar Mistakes
page 222

 4.3 page 222

For many companies ~~competed~~ *competing* in today's global market, a diverse workforce is one strategy to increase success, but there are challenges. Some businesses ~~recruited~~ *recruiting* people from different backgrounds believe it increases creativity, but it can increase conflict, too. While employees with diverse backgrounds offer ~~perspectives unique~~ *unique perspectives* on problems, they may also be unable to see each other's points of view. Ted Park, ~~is~~ a management consultant, says that employees must be trained to work together. Some ~~employees upset~~ *upset employees* can cause additional problems and conflicts. Training on cultural diversity ~~giving~~ *given* regularly is more effective than training that is given once. Companies ~~thought~~ *thinking* about diversifying their workforce should prepare carefully for it.

Ⓒ Avoiding Plagiarism page 223

 4.4 page 224

1 There are two reasons:
   a She lacked skill and didn't know what to do.
   b She gave in to temptation instead of saying no.

2 *Possible answers:*
   a She could ask her instructor for help right away. She could ask a classmate to help her.
   b She could turn off her phone while she is studying. She could study and not check Facebook.

 4.5 page 224

Answers will vary.

(8) ARGUMENTATIVE ESSAYS 2

GLOBAL STUDIES: ISSUES IN GLOBALIZATION

Page 229

1 a (*Possible answer:* A group's success depends on how its members work together.)

2 *Possible answer:* In 2014 and 2015, there was an Ebola epidemic in Africa. Many other countries including the United States, Great Britain, and France came together to fight it and treat people.

1 PREPARE YOUR IDEAS

B Reflect on the Topic page 230

1.1 page 230

Possible answers:
GOOD:
• there is more innovation
• people can buy many convenient things to make their lives easier
BAD:
• makes people compare their lives and feel dissatisfied
• companies make money but people get poorer

2 EXPAND YOUR KNOWLEDGE

A Academic Vocabulary page 232

2.1 pages 232–233

1 a	3 a	5 b	7 b
2 b	4 a	6 a	8 b

B Academic Phrases page 233

2.2 page 233

1 a   2 b   3 b

C Writing in the Real World page 234
Possible answers:

According to the author, population growth is causing global warming and mass extinction of animals. The author might discuss information on the amount of population growth and give examples of species that are now extinct or declining in numbers.

2.3 page 235

Possible answers:

1 It could hurt the economy because fewer people are working, which reduces the amount of money for government and social programs.

2 Because when people talk about overpopulation, they need to discuss sensitive human-rights issues, including reproduction and cultural values, and it is hard to agree on them.

3 McKee and Mora want scientists to start addressing and discussing the overpopulation issue in their work so that more people are aware of the problem. Mora would also like an education campaign. I think that overpopulation is important to discuss, but every culture must make their own decisions about what to do because we will never agree to one solution.

2.4 page 235

Possible answers:

1 The writer gives as evidence a study done by Jeffrey McKee of Ohio State University.

2 Geographer Camilo Mora of the University of Hawaii argues against the idea in paragraph 6 that slowing population growth would hurt the economy. He says that if population grows, the resulting lack of jobs for young people can lead to social unrest. I think that this strengthens Hance's argument because it gives a negative effect of overpopulation.

3 The prediction that is mentioned is that the world's population will peak at 9 to 10 billion by mid-century. Hance disagrees, saying such estimates are optimistic. The writer does not, however, offer any evidence, so it does not seem very convincing.

3 STUDY ACADEMIC WRITING

A Student Model page 236

1 Circled words and phrases: *consumer society, new goods,* and *owning.*

   The essay prompt is asking the writer to argue if a consumer society is good or bad for the world.

2 *Possible answer:* I think that the writer will argue against a consumer society because in the title he says it's time to rethink our consumer society.

Analyze Writing Skills   pages 236–237

1 Circled: a, b, c

2 Underlined: A consumer society is not good for the world because it leads to unhappiness and it destroys natural resources and the environment.

3 examples ("Soon after … they look for a new product to buy"); personal experience ("In my country, the Dominican Republic …"); facts (According to journalist and best-selling author …")

4 Circled: b

5 Circled: b

 3.1 page 238

1 The purpose of the essay is to convince the reader that a consumer society is not good for the world.

2 *Possible answer:* The second reason – how a consumer society uses up natural resources and contributes to pollution – is the stronger reason because the facts help you see the impact of it on the environment and plant and animal species.

3 *Possible answer:* I think a consumer society is not good for society. I think people care too much about what they have. They spend too much time thinking about getting and having things. Sometimes I feel that I am part of a consumer society, but I try to stop myself. I don't want to get in debt. I don't want money and things to be the center of my life.

 3.2 pages 238–239

I Introductory paragraph
   Thesis statement: A consumer society is not good for the world because it leads to unhappiness and it depletes natural resources and pollutes the environment.

II Leads to unhappiness
   A Happy feeling does not last long
      1 Consumers feel regret or disappointment
      2 Terrible cycle
   B Money cannot buy happiness
      1 Ex: Dominican Republic story
      2 Malcom Gladwell

III Uses up valuable natural resources and causes pollution
   A UN Environment Programme: average person – 16 tons of natural resources
      1 Level is not sustainable
   B Negative effect on animal species
      1 Climate change: 40% of species extinct by 2050

IV Consumer society – important for economic growth
   A Creates jobs and income
   B Economy will fail, worldwide crisis
   C Cost is too high
      1 Creating jobs and products without responsibility is bad

V Concluding paragraph

B Argumentation with Refutation
   page 239

 3.3 page 240

1 Two paragraphs build the student writer's argument.

2 One strength of the counterargument is that a consumer society does create jobs. The weakness of a consumer society is that it destroys the environment.

 3.4 page 241

Answers will vary.

 3.6 page 243

Thesis Statement: A consumer society is not good for the world because it leads to unhappiness and it destroys natural resources and the environment.

Topic Sentence for Body Paragraph 1: People in a consumer society crave the latest clothes and electronic devices to make them happy, but that happiness does not last.

Topic Sentence for Body Paragraph 2: A consumer society also rapidly uses up natural resources and causes pollution.

 3.7 page 244

1 Example

2 Example

3 Fact

4 Quotation

5 Statistic

6 Personal experience

3.8 page 245

1 According to the Hunger Project, a child dies from hunger-related diseases every 10 seconds.
2 Recently in the news, a very popular high-school student was killed because he did not want to join a gang.
3 Benjamin Franklin said, "An investment in knowledge pays the best interest."

 3.10 pages 246–247

Possible answers:

2 Some opponents say that our economy will suffer as our population ages. There will not be enough workers for jobs. An example is Japan.
3 Critics may argue that people should focus on solving local problems, not international ones. The reason they give for this is that an individual cannot make a big difference when the problem is a global one.
4 Some experts claim that fighting global warming will harm the world economy. They feel businesses will not be able to remain competitive.
5 Some people say that the United Nations is not effective. They call the agency useless and unable to deal quickly with global problems.

 3.11 page 247

Possible answers:

2 Some opponents say that our economy will suffer as our population ages. There will not be enough workers for jobs. An example is Japan. This is only partly true. People are living longer and have better health, so they will continue to work longer.
3 Critics may argue that people should focus on solving local problems, not international ones. The reason they give for this is that an individual cannot make a big difference when the problem is a global one. This seems credible, but the opposite is true. People can make a huge difference. For example, I give to a charity that pays for all of the school supplies in a poor classroom.
4 Some experts claim that fighting global warming will harm the world economy. They feel businesses will not be able to remain competitive. While this may be true up to a point, research has shown that businesses that have to use greener technologies actually become much more competitive in time.

5 Some people say that the United Nations is not effective. They call the agency useless and unable to deal quickly with global problems. There is some truth to this. However, for every case where the U.N. didn't act there are many cases where they were able to stop a conflict, enforce an agreement, or provide humanitarian aid to refugees.

 3.13 page 248

Possible answers:

1 Yes, it is memorable because he challenges governments to show responsibility and be brave.
2 Yes, because he provided a lot of strong evidence.

4 SHARPEN YOUR SKILLS

A Writing Skill 1: Avoiding Faulty Logic page 249

 4.1 page 249

Possible answers:

Almost everyone
~~Everyone~~ agrees that clean water is the most serious issue facing the world. According to a recent report by the World Health Organization, 1.7 million people die each year from diseases that come from unsafe water. ~~No one thinks~~ *Few people think* that governments are doing enough to make companies stop polluting the environment, *almost nobody* but ~~nobody~~ complains. Companies ~~never~~ *hardly ever* clean up the pollution that they create, and they ~~always~~ *often* try to avoid paying fines, too.

 4.2 page 250

Check: 1, 3, 5

B Writing Skill 2: Sentence Variety page 251

ACTIVITY 4.3 page 251

Possible answer:

It is crucial that people have safe air to breathe. Poor air quality can make people sick or lead to more serious health issues, even death. Many countries have problems with air pollution. A recent *New York Times* article by Wong stated that there are 1.2 million deaths caused by air pollution per year in China. In Beijing the smog is especially bad, and for many years, officials have been trying to clean it. In 2014, Beijing held a marathon race, which attracted over 25,000 runners. Although many runners finished the race, some did not because they were having trouble breathing. Beijing has taken steps to reduce its air pollution, but there is still much to do.

C Grammar for Writing: Modals for Hedging page 252

ACTIVITY 4.4 page 252

1 must   3 can   5 might
2 will   4 should   6 may

Avoiding Common Mistakes page 253

ACTIVITY 4.5 page 253

In conclusion, there are certain things that we
            do
must ~~doing~~ to end poverty. People need enough
                              will
food to eat. If they do not eat, they ~~would~~ not
have the energy to be productive. They also must
have a quality education. This means they should
  go
~~going~~ to school every day and continue their
                        should not quit
studies when they get older. They ~~should quit not~~
during harvest time or when their families need
                                    will
help with work. If they quit school, they ~~would~~
probably not get a good job later. Finally, people
                              have
need a way to make money so they can ~~having~~
economic security. If people have these three
                  will not have
things together, they ~~not will have~~ to live a life in
poverty. They should be able to break the cycle
of poverty.

D Avoiding Plagiarism page 254

ACTIVITY 4.6 page 255

Check: 1, 2

1 Underlined: Researchers have found that plastics are a significant source of death for sea animals.

2 Underlined: Several specialists who work with women in developing countries have shown that educating women leads to healthier and more financially strong families. Koppell and Sperling both found that education reduced the number of infants who die in poor families. AND They also mention that the quality of education is important to have positive results.

NAME: ....

DATE: ....

Part A: Academic Vocabulary

Circle the correct words to complete the sentences.

One local leader has suggested starting **cooperation / community / source** vegetable gardens.
(1)
She said the vegetable gardens would increase **scope / basis / cooperation** and offer a local food
(2)
supply / transition / community. They would also help with the mayor's big plan to have
(3)
sufficient / supplied / based fresh vegetables for everyone in the city by the end of the year. The leader
(4)
wants to use an old parking lot for the first new garden. Making the **community / scope / transition** from
(5)
a parking lot to a vegetable garden would require digging up concrete, planting soil, and arranging for a
reliable **source / basis / cooperation** of water. Eventually, she wants the **supply / scope / transition** of the
(6)   (7)
campaign to change most of the city's unused public lands to gardens. The **basis / community / sufficiency**
(8)
for this proposal of neighborhood vegetable gardens is that it would improve the overall health of the people
in the city.

Part B: Academic Collocations

Complete the sentences with the academic collocations in the box. Use the correct form of the phrases.

limited supply	on a daily basis	sense of community	water supply	wide scope

1 The Environmental Protection Agency is responsible for making sure that the ....
   in the U.S. is clean and safe to drink.

2 Shared activities in one's neighborhood, such as working at a local garden, can help groups of people
   develop a ....

3 Since there is a .... of fossil fuels, some governments are promoting the use of
   alternative sources of energy, such as solar power.

4 One thing everyone can do .... to help the environment is turn off the lights when
   leaving a room.

5 The field of environmental studies includes a .... of topics, ranging from wildlife
   protection to climate change.

NAME: ....   DATE: ....

Part A

Complete the sentences with the infinitive form of the verbs in the box.

call	preserve	volunteer	convert	recycle	waste

1 The neighborhood environmental group wants .... the old parking lot into a public garden.

2 Local leaders must stop development in the nearby wooded areas .... their beautiful old trees.

3 The mayor decided .... Sundays "bike day" as a way to encourage residents to ride bikes instead of drive.

4 The city is providing residents with large containers .... plastic, glass, and paper.

5 It's a good idea not .... water, especially in places where there is little rainfall.

6 As a community-service project, the high-school seniors decided .... to clean the beach on Saturday.

Part B

Correct the mistake with the infinitive in each sentence.

1 The Environmental Studies professors discussed to hold classes in a city park so students would get a first-hand view of the local environment.

2 When gas prices decrease, people tend to not buy hybrid cars.

3 Many grocery stores no longer provide plastic bags for help save the environment.

NAME: .... DATE: ....

Part A

Read the original passage and the paraphrased student texts below. Circle the number of the plagiarized student text.

Original Passage:

The Timken Museum, located in San Diego's historic Balboa Park, is being recognized for reducing its energy use by more than 50%, preventing more than 80 metric tons of greenhouse gas emissions from being released into the environment. As part of its effort to reduce energy use, the museum converted 50-year-old light fixtures to advanced LED lighting and installed new timers, dimmers, and sensors.

Source: "EPA Administrator Gina McCarthy, Mayor Kevin Faulconer Recognize Timken Museum for Reducing Energy Use by more than 50%." *Environmental Protection Agency.* 18 May 2015. Web. 20 May 2015.

1 **Student Text A:**

According to a report from the U.S. EPA, 80 metric tons of greenhouse gases have been prevented from leaking into the atmosphere by San Diego's Timken Museum's recent effort. The museum has decreased its energy use by at least 50% through using LED light sensors, timers, and dimmers instead of traditional incandescent lighting.

2 **Student Text B:**

As part of its effort to reduce energy use, the Timken Museum, located in San Diego's historic Balboa Park, converted 50-year-old light fixtures to advanced LED lighting and installed new timers, dimmers, and sensors. The museum is being recognized for reducing its energy use by more than 50%, preventing more than 80 metric tons of greenhouse gas emissions from being released into the environment.

(CONTINUED)

NAME: ....   DATE: ....

Part B

Read the original passage and the plagiarized student texts below. Underline the phrases and sentences that the students plagiarized.

Original Passage:

In January 2013, air quality in Beijing and several other major cities reached record lows, and the public is increasingly taking note of this issue. Nearly half (47%) rate air pollution a very big problem, an increase of 11 percentage points from 2012. And following a year that included headlines about thousands of dead pigs floating down a river through the center of Shanghai, concerns about water pollution have also increased. Four-in-ten say it is a very big problem, compared with 33% in 2012.

Source: "Environmental Concerns on the Rise in China." *Pew Research Center.* 19 Sept. 2013. Web. 20 May 2015.

1 **Student Text A:**

Air quality in Beijing and several other major cities reached record lows, and the public is increasingly taking note of this issue. In an increase of 11 percentage points from 2012, nearly half (47%) rate air pollution a very big problem. Forty percent say water pollution is also a concern, after thousands of dead pigs floating down a river through the center of Shanghai.

2 **Student Text B:**

Air and water pollution are concerns in China. In January 2013, air quality in major Chinese cities reached record lows. Forty-seven percent think air pollution is a very big problem, which is up 11% from 2012. And following a year that included headlines about thousands of dead pigs floating down a river through the center of Shanghai, concerns about water pollution have also increased. Four-in-ten say it is a very big problem, compared with 33% in 2012.

Instructors: This is a list of possible prompts to assign as a unit writing quiz.

1 Many institutions, such as hospitals, universities, and public buildings, are environmentally conscious; however, some are not. What steps can institutions take in order to become more environmentally conscious?

2 What are three ways that individuals can save water? Give examples.

3 Think of three ways that one institution, such as a school, store, or building, can save energy. Explain.

4 What efforts do you think the government can make to help limit air pollution? Explain.

5 Do you think it is the responsibility of individuals, institutions, the government, or all three to look after the environment? Explain.

NAME: .... DATE: ....

Part A: Academic Vocabulary

Circle the correct words and phrases to complete the sentences.

1 To apply for a teaching position with Longmire College, candidates must submit an essay about their **persistent / fundamental / expected** beliefs about education.

2 Many parents **assume / rely on / persist** that extra homework helps their children learn more; however, studies show that this may not be true.

3 High-school students can often **rely on / assume / expect** their teachers for extra help outside of class, but in college they need to be more independent.

4 Professor Martin has high **persistence / gap / expectations** of his students: he wants all of his students to rewrite their essays until they receive a grade of "A."

5 The writing **gap / factor / task** was so complicated that Mario had to divide it into several more manageable steps.

6 One **factor / fundamental / expectation** college students should consider when choosing a major is the job market for graduates.

7 Because of the **task / gap / persistence** in math and science achievement between the United States and China, many American school districts have changed their curriculum.

8 After much **task / expectation / persistence**, the director of studies finally convinced the dean to adopt the new curriculum.

Part B: Academic Phrases

Read the paragraph. Then match each phrase with the reason that the writer used it.

Many think that learning a second language as a child is easier than learning one as an adult. However, **according to** Professor Ruth Whitcomb of Dolman College, this is not necessarily true. **As she points out in** her article "Go For It: Learn a Second Language!," 78% of adult second-language learners she surveyed feel successful in their second-language studies. **While some may argue** that children may be less inhibited than adults while learning a second language, Professor Whitcomb contends that this is not the case. In fact, she encourages even more adults to learn a second language.

PHRASE	REASON
☐ 1 according to	a to introduce an author and article
☐ 2 as she points out in	b to introduce an opposing idea
☐ 3 while some may argue that	c to introduce an author and her ideas

NAME: ....   DATE: ....

Part A

Add *that* to the correct place in each sentence.

1 Teachers typically believe students learn better when they are interested in the material.

2 The researchers concluded most children who read extensively become better writers.

3 Education experts argue studying multiple disciplines such as math, science, languages, and the arts, results in more well-balanced students.

4 The claim standardized testing, such as the ACT or SAT, does not measure academic ability is debatable.

Part B

These sentences are from an academic essay. Correct the mistake in each sentence.

1 Many parents think that children spending too much time on computers in school these days.

2 Maria told her education professor that would write her paper on learning technology.

3 Studies show experiential learning (i.e., learning by doing) can benefit many students.

NAME: ....   DATE: ....

Read the original passage and the paraphrases. Circle the paraphrasing strategy used in each paraphrase.

Original Passage:

Students learn better when they have an interest in the subject they are learning about. Fifty-eight percent of history majors at Waltham University said they decided to major in history only after taking introductory history courses in freshman year. (Summers 102)

Paraphrase 1:

Over half of the students at Waltham University decided to major in history after they took history in their first year of college. Summers says that this indicates that students are motivated to learn when they like the subject they are taking. (102)

a use synonyms

b break up or change order of ideas

c change word forms

Paraphrase 2:

According to Summers, students who are interested in the subject they take learn better. In fact, 58% of students majoring in history at Waltham University said they chose to major in history after taking introduction to history courses in their first year. (102)

a use synonyms

b break up or change order of ideas

c change word forms

Paraphrase 3:

Students tend to be more successful if they like the subject they are studying. Summers says that almost 60% of history majors at Waltham University chose history as a major after their first-year history classes.

a use synonyms

b break up or change order of ideas

c change word forms

Instructors: This is a list of possible prompts to assign as a unit writing quiz.

1 Think of two different teachers you have had. Was one method more interesting or effective for you? Compare their teaching methods using block organization and the same points of comparison.

2 Some students prefer to study alone. Others prefer to study in a study group. Compare the advantages and disadvantages using block organization and the same points of comparison.

3 Think of two schools you are familiar with. Consider such points of comparison as student support, student population, facilities, and the general school environment. Compare the schools using block organization. Do you prefer one more than the other?

4 Compare learning with traditional print textbooks and learning with electronic books. What are the advantages and disadvantages? Use block organization and the same points of comparison.

5 Which do you prefer as a learner – doing group work or working independently? Why? Use block organization and the same points of comparison.

NAME: ....   DATE: ....

Part A: Academic Vocabulary

Circle the correct words to complete the sentences.

1 People with a strong sense of community will more easily **survive / participate / adapt** a difficult situation.

2 Community groups that hold social events for people without families often have a big **network / framework / impact** on them.

3 Having a large **framework / impact / network** of friends is important for some people; for others, having only a few close friends is all they need.

4 If a community has the **infrastructure / impact / survival** to support all of its residents during a crisis, fewer people will have communication, transportation, or health-care problems.

5 Two people who have an **adaptable / identical / impactful** problem, such as losing a job, may handle the problem very differently.

6 Studies show that people who **participate / survive / adapt** in volunteer activities, such as fundraising or food drives, benefit both themselves and their community.

7 New residents of a city can **survive / participate / adapt** to their new environment more easily by joining local social groups.

8 A successful community group must have a strong **network / impact / framework**, such as good organization, management, and budget.

Part B: Academic Collocations

Complete the sentences with the correct form of the academic collocations in the box.

an extensive network	have an impact	nearly identical
social impact	social network	

1 Last year, Mayor Martinez .... on his city because he lowered city taxes and the unemployment rate.

2 .... are important for community organizers because they depend on a help from a wide range of friends and acquaintances.

3 .... of volunteers is needed when there is a major disaster or tragedy.

4 Even though the two public gardens look ...., they are very different: one of them is tended by professional gardeners, while the other is cared for by volunteers.

5 More funding for programs such as helping the poor and homeless would have a huge .... on the community.

NAME: ....   DATE: ....

Part A

Underline the identifying relative clauses and circle the relative pronouns in the sentences.

1 Neighborhoods that hold monthly parties or events have a strong sense of community.

2 The doctor who volunteers at the clinic likes to help the needy.

3 The School Supply Bank collects school supplies for parents who do not have enough money to buy them for their children.

4 The city leader whom Mrs. Delfano called promised to help her organization raise money.

5 Children whose parents show self-discipline typically have a strong work ethic in school.

6 Sibling relationships that are strong in childhood often remain strong in adulthood.

Part B

Circle the correct relative pronouns to complete the paragraph.

Neighbors **which / who / whose** are friendly to their fellow neighbors are not necessarily out of date.
(1)
A few decades ago, you could find a great place to live in the suburbs **where / which / that** people made
(2)
friends with other people on their street or in their building. You can probably imagine 1960s neighbors

to **where / that / whom** a weekly Friday-night party was the norm. On the other hand, in some modern
(3)
suburban neighborhoods, you might find people **who / which / where** live on the same street not talking to
(4)
each other. However, this is not true in smaller communities. In smaller towns, you may find neighbors

who / which / where regularly get together. This trend is beginning to extend to more densely populated
(5)
areas. In suburbs and even cities, more neighbors are finding ways to become more social with each other,

where / which / who makes them feel a strong sense of community, safety, and friendship.
(6)

NAME: ....   DATE: ....

Part A

Check (✓) the sentences that are common knowledge.

☐ 1 Thousand of people died in Nepal's powerful 2015 earthquakes.

☐ 2 Hurricane Andrew was the third-strongest hurricane to hit the United States.

☐ 3 If a community has a strong infrastructure, it can help in times of natural disasters.

☐ 4 There is a water shortage in California as there has been little rain since 2010.

☐ 5 The likelihood that a tornado reaches the worst category (F5) is less than 0.1%.

Part B:

Check (✓) the situations in which the students need to use citations.

☐ 1 Marta is writing an essay about workers' rights in the early 20th century. She learned from many sources that President Theodore Roosevelt was in support of unions.

☐ 2 Gabriel is researching community organizing. He interviewed the head of a non-profit organization in his city.

☐ 3 Sandy needs to write an essay about the coral reef in the Caribbean. She wants to include data from studies on the health of the reefs.

☐ 4 Alexandra wants to write a paper about the benefits of exercise. She read several publications that claim people should find ways to exercise to stay healthy.

☐ 5 For his paper on community outreach, Leo wants to include the local police chief's opinion on whether police officers should participate in community events.

Instructors: This is a list of possible prompts to assign as a unit writing quiz.

1 Think of two distinct cities. Compare and contrast them using three different points of comparison such as friendliness, cost of living, and things to do. Give examples.

2 Compare and contrast living in a big city and a small city. Discuss such factors as feeling of community, cost of living, and safety. Use point-by-point comparison.

3 Think of a country you know well. Compare and contrast how the country was at a time in the past with how it is today. Discuss three different points of comparison, such as traditions, attitudes toward family, and ways to make a living.

4 Compare two similar places in the community (e.g., stores, restaurants, community centers, or parks). Discuss the similarities and differences using three different points of comparison.

5 Think of two community organizations. Consider the type of help each provides, the people they help, and the people who work or volunteer there. Compare them using three points of comparison.

NAME: ....

DATE: ....

Part A: Academic Vocabulary

Circle the correct words to complete the sentences.

1 Some people in older **scenarios / generations / perspectives** think that children should not be online.

2 From the **perspective / scenario / generation** of some single adults, visiting an online dating site is preferable to meeting potential partners in nightclubs.

3 Developing online friendships **enables / promotes / perceives** many shy children to make friends more easily.

4 The Internet can help children become more **inherent / ongoing / aware** of different cultures, so that they can understand them more easily.

5 Learning about other cultures in school may **promote / perceive / enable** tolerance and respect for others.

6 In the present day, listening to music while surfing the Internet and texting friends is an everyday **generation / perspective / scenario** for most school-age children.

7 Over the last several years, there has been an **ongoing / aware / inherent** debate about Internet safety, especially among children.

8 If children are taught at a young age about the **aware / inherent / generational** dangers of online sharing, they will be more careful when using technology.

Part B: Academic Phrases

Complete the sentences with the correct form of the academic phrases in the box.

another impact of	as a result of	one effect of

Social media has affected the way people share their ideas. .... social media is that
(1)
users are more aware of other people's views. For example, people often use social-networking sites to share

their opinions about politics or current events. .... social media is that it has led to
(2)
positive social change across the globe. For example, after recent natural disasters, non-profit organizations

have used websites to ask the public for help. Despite its criticisms, many positive things have occurred

.... social media.
(3)

NAME: ....   DATE: ....

Part A

Complete the sentences with the correct forms of the verbs in parentheses.

1 If job seekers .... their personal views online, some companies
   (post)
   .... them.
   (not hire)

2 Online class discussion boards .... useful if students ....
   (be)   (contribute)
   to them in meaningful ways.

3 When a newspaper .... its opinion pieces online, many readers
   (publish)
   .... their reactions.
   (post)

4 Sofia .... more customers to her yarn shop if she ....
   (attract)   (share)
   positive customer experiences on her website.

5 Sharing personal information over the Internet .... risky if you
   (be)
   .... a secure Internet connection.
   (not have)

6 Candidates for the next election .... more attention from the public if they
   (receive)
   .... online communities such as Facebook or Twitter.
   (join)

7 When students .... drafts of their essays with each other online, they
   (share)
   .... peer feedback more quickly.
   (get)

8 If children .... unlimited access to the Internet, they ....
   (have)   (find)
   inappropriate websites for youngsters.

Part B

Correct the mistake in each sentence.

1 If children will use social media too much, they might post pictures of themselves they might later regret.

2 Restaurant and hotel owners can attract more customers if they uploads videos of successful events on social-media sites.

3 If students want to respond privately to a professor's message to the entire class they should not hit the "reply all" button.

4 When students take online classes, they will be able to take the class anywhere and when they take online classes they will meet people from all over the world.

5 Posting photos and updates on social-media sites is a good way to keep in touch, if your family and friends live far away.

NAME: ....

DATE: ....

Part A

Circle the things that are needed for each type of citation.

1 In-text citations for print sources:

   a author

   b date

   c page number

2 In-text citations for web sources:

   a author

   b date

   c page number

3 Works Cited List:

   a works in alphabetical order

   b one entry per author

   c page number

   d year of publication

Part B

Check (✓) the citation that is formatted correctly.

1 In-text print source citation:

   ☐ a Sharing everything online can have both positive and negative effects. Most notable are the negative effects, such as getting a loan or a job. (Stanhope 54).

   ☐ b Sharing everything online can have both positive and negative effects. Stanhope says the most notable effects are negative, such as getting a loan or a job.

2 In-text web source citation:

   ☐ a Over 90% of Americans polled want control over who collects information about them, and what information is collected (Madden and Rainie).

   ☐ b According to an article on online sharing, over 90% of Americans polled want control over who collects information about them, and what information is collected (2015).

3 Works Cited citation:

   ☐ a Belk, Russell. "You are what you can access: Sharing and collaborative consumption online." *Journal of Business Research* 67.8 (2014): 1595–1600. Web.

   ☐ b Belk, Russell. "You are what you can access: Sharing and collaborative consumption online." *Journal of Business Research* 67.8 (2014): 1595–1600. Web. 20 May 2015.

Instructors: This is a list of possible prompts to assign as a unit writing quiz.

1 Many people use smartphones nowadays, some more often than others. What effects does using smartphones regularly have on people's lives and society in general?

2 Some teachers have a policy against using cell phones in class. Discuss the positive and negative effects of this policy.

3 What causes people to continuously post pictures and updates on social-media sites, such as Facebook, Twitter, and Flickr?

4 Think of one device you use a lot (e.g., a cell phone, GPS, or tablet computer). What are the effects of using the device on a regular basis?

5 Rating and reviewing restaurants, doctors, hair stylists, and professors online has become popular. What are the effects of this practice?

NAME: ....   DATE: ....

Part A: Academic Vocabulary

Circle the correct words and phrases to complete the paragraph.

Maintaining a healthy work-life balance has become **a global / a conscious / an experimental** issue lately.
(1)
Researchers in the United States, Europe, and Asia have conducted **urges / senses / experiments** on how
(2)
people's working life affects their overall happiness. They found that when people **ensure / focus / consume**
(3)
mainly on work and don't spend enough time with their families, they feel more guilt and stress. They stated

that people should be **experimental / global / conscious** of the fact that work is only one aspect of life.
(4)
In fact, being good at a job does not **focus / consume / ensure** happiness. In addition, people should not
(5)
let the **urge / sense / experiment** to work be so strong that it controls their lives; living to work rather
(6)
than working to live makes little **experiment / sense / urge**. When work **consumes / ensures / focuses**
(7)   (8)
too much time and energy, it can only lead to severe stress and depression. They concluded that finding an

appropriate work-life balance is essential to lower stress and more happiness.

Part B: Academic Collocations

Complete the sentences with the correct form of the academic collocations in the box.

conduct an experiment	the main focus of	make a conscious decision
make sense	a strong urge	

1 .... a recent Pew Research Center report was work-life balance in different kinds
   of work.

2 Last year, the A-Tech Games Corporation .... to allow employees to work at home
   at least one day a week.

3 Although she had .... to check her email on the weekend, Teresa did not check her
   messages until Monday morning.

4 The researchers .... to find out whether allowing employees to wear casual clothes
   every day would increase productivity.

5 It .... for employees to eat lunch away from their desks because they are more
   productive in the afternoons.

NAME: .... DATE: ....

Part A

Complete the sentences with the correct reporting verbs.

1 Research **shows / believes** that parents find raising children more rewarding than working, but also more tiring.

2 The psychologists **described / concluded** that more people prefer not to work on the weekends.

3 Dr. Wyatt **suggested / presented** the results of her work-life balance survey to the experts.

4 The author **describes / argues** that mothers who work can be happy raising children and holding full-time jobs.

5 Some studies **found / explained** that children whose mothers do not work perform better in school.

6 The speaker **gave / recommended** the audience three tips on how to achieve a healthy approach to work.

Part B

Correct the mistakes in the passage. There is one mistake in each sentence. Some sentences may have more than one correct answer.

(1) Most research says the majority of workers seem content in their jobs. (2) However, Landry, in his independent study on work satisfaction, found only 46% of those whom he interviewed were happy with their jobs. (3) Participants in Landry's study described that difficulties in trying to find satisfaction in their current jobs. (4) Landry concluded while his study was small, the results were significant enough to give reason for further research.

NAME: ....

DATE: ....

Part A

Match the website addresses with the type of sources they are.

- [ ] 1 www.cnn.com
- [ ] 2 www.smithsonian.org
- [ ] 3 www.baylor.edu
- [ ] 4 www.hhs.gov

- a government website
- b company website
- c non-profit website
- d educational institution

Part B

Check (✓) the reliable sources for use in a research paper about modern parenting.

- [ ] 1 A scholarly article about working mothers' attitudes toward childcare at www.smithsonian.org
- [ ] 2 An article by a university sociology professor on working single parents at www.baylor.edu
- [ ] 3 A new story about recent celebrities' parenting styles at www.cnn.com
- [ ] 4 An article on working parents from the U.S. Health and Human Services website (www.hhs.gov)
- [ ] 5 An article from a company that sells parenting and childcare advice at www.parentchildtoday.com

Instructors: This is a copy of "A Tax on Unhealthy Foods" from pages 144–145 of the Student's Book. The students have already read it in class. You can assign it as a unit writing quiz with the following directions:

1 Read the article again and annotate it.
2 Write a summary. Use your own ideas.

A Tax on Unhealthy Foods

by Michelle Embrich

There is a crisis[1] today in the United States. It is not a political crisis. It is not an economic crisis. It is a health care crisis. Simply put: Too many people are overweight, and the impact on the economy could be disastrous.

The overweight American, fairly rare when I was growing up in the 1970s, is now the norm. In fact, according to the results of a 2014 study cited in the Harvard School of Public Health Obesity Prevention Source, over two-thirds of adults are overweight or obese. Overweight and obese people are not only a danger to themselves, living shorter, unhealthy lives; but they also put a strain[2] on the country's health care system and make health care costs and health insurance higher for everyone. I propose a simple solution: put a tax on foods that are high in fat and high in sugar. This tax on unhealthy foods would reduce the number of unhealthily overweight people and keep health care costs from rising.

Would a tax on unhealthy foods be effective? Absolutely. First, we have a history of successfully discouraging unhealthy habits by putting a high price tag on them. For instance, high taxes on tobacco worked to reduce the number of smokers in the United States. People were less likely to buy cigarettes – or simply bought fewer than usual – because they did not want to spend more money on them. It seems likely that our food habits would change just as our cigarette habits did. Second, research shows that if a tax of 18 percent were put on soda and pizza alone, the average American could lose five pounds (*Archives of Internal Medicine*). Imagine how much more weight could be lost if hamburgers and fries were taxed, too.

The bigger question is whether a tax like this one would be politically acceptable. Probably not – because Americans traditionally don't like the government to interfere in their private lives. One example is the unsuccessful attempt to ban[3] oversized sodas in New York City restaurants. The public was outraged.[4] "We don't like being bossed around by the government," residents said. "This is becoming a nanny state,"[5] they argued. In fact, a poll by NBC found that as many as 6 in 10

[1]**crisis:** extremely dangerous or difficult situation
[2]**strain:** something that causes problems or makes a situation more difficult
[3]**ban:** forbid the use or sale of something
[4]**outraged:** very angry or shocked
[5]**nanny state:** a view that government has too much control over people's choices

(CONTINUED)

New Yorkers felt that the ban was a bad idea. Similarly, an April 2012 national survey on a related topic found that only 28 percent of Americans said that they would support taxing high-fat and high-sugar food. It is also likely true that the companies that make those foods would not want that, either.

However, while Americans dislike government interference in their private lives, they might agree to a tax if they had to pay higher taxes. Today, the annual cost of obesity-related health care in the United States is estimated by some researchers to be $190 billion, or 20 percent of the total health care costs in the country. It is expected to almost double by 2030. It won't be long before there are more and more people saying: "Why didn't the government do more to combat this economic crisis?"

A tax on unhealthy foods, combined with subsidizing[6] the cost of healthy foods, is inevitably[7] in America's future. It will save lives and reduce the rising cost of health care. We must admit that for this crisis, the freedom to eat fast foods is not worth fighting for because many of us will not live long lives if we win it.

[6]**subsidize:** give money as part of the cost to encourage something
[7]**inevitably:** in a way that cannot be avoided

NAME: ....   DATE: ....

Part A: Academic Vocabulary

Circle the correct words to complete the sentences.

1 Research shows that being bilingual – for **instance / interaction / emphasis**, being able to speak both German and Portuguese – has a positive effect on the brain.

2 When speakers **interact / shift / ignore** from speaking one language to another, they often begin thinking in that language.

3 Dr. Martin thinks schools should **emphasize / ignore / interact** foreign-language instruction so students can communicate in different cultures.

4 What some cultures consider **various / shifting / appropriate** behavior may be regarded as rude or unacceptable in other cultures.

5 It's important not to **ignore / emphasize / interact** the social rules of a country you are visiting; if you do, you might insult its residents.

6 Linguists study **appropriate / various / interactive** languages to help them understand patterns in similar language groups.

7 Many U.S. cities provide **instances / shifts / immigrants** with English-language classes to help them adjust to their new society.

8 When newcomers to a country **ignore / interact / emphasize** with local people, they usually learn about their new culture more quickly.

Part B: Academic Phrases

Complete the paragraph with the correct form of the academic phrases in the box.

the fact that	for this reason	in part

Despite the increased number of immigrant children in U.S. schools, many schools are moving away from offering bilingual education programs. .... fewer schools have bilingual education
(1)
is, ..., due to funding problems. Budget cuts have led school administrators to limit
(2)
programs that are not considered absolutely necessary. ...., many volunteers are
(3)
offering these students additional language help in free after-school programs at community centers.

NAME: ....

DATE: ....

Part A

Complete the sentences with the correct passive form of the verb in parentheses.

1 Bilingual classes .... at many Springfield schools nowadays.
   (offer)

2 Students at Merriweather High School .... the choice of studying French
   (give)
   or Chinese.

3 Multicultural training .... for all new employees of LNT International Corporation.
   (require)

4 Yesterday, the new students .... to the welcome party by their teachers.
   (invite)

5 Marta .... by her boss to take Spanish classes to help her communicate better
   (encourage)
   with Spanish-speaking clients.

6 Mindy .... to represent her country at the college multicultural seminar.
   (choose)

Part B

Correct the mistake in each sentence.

1 Last Monday, Professor Harte's students was tested on relative clauses.

2 Arabic and Japanese are been taught in Sydney public schools.

3 François was glad that the spelling rules was posted on the wall of his classroom.

4 The cross-cultural curriculum was helped students understand different cultures.

5 The bilingual curriculum is been adopted by most of the schools in the area.

NAME: ....

DATE: ....

Part A

Complete the note-taking steps with the words from the box.

code	notes	organize	source	understanding

1 Write .... information on a piece of paper, in an electronic document, or on a notecard.

2 Read to get a general .... of the main ideas. Underline repeated words that may be important.

3 Read again for the main idea and key points, and begin to make .... If needed, include page numbers where you found them.

4 Color- .... the information on your cards to avoid plagiarizing as you write. For example, highlight quotes, paraphrases, and your own ideas in different colors.

5 .... your notes well. For example, alphabetize them by last name of the author.

Part B

Read the excerpt from an original source and a student's notes. Check (✓) the problems with the student's notes.

Excerpt from Original Source:

A record 33.2 million Hispanics in the U.S. speak English proficiently, according to a new Pew Research Center analysis of U.S. Census Bureau data.[1] In 2013, this group made up 68% of all Hispanics ages 5 and older, up from 59% in 2000.

At the same time that the share of Latinos who speak English proficiently is growing, the share that speaks Spanish at home has been declining over the last 13 years. In 2013, 73% of Latinos ages 5 and older said they speak Spanish at home, down from 78% who said the same in 2000. Despite this decline, a record 35.8 million Hispanics speak Spanish at home, a number that has continued to increase as the nation's Hispanic population has grown.

Source: Krogstad, Jens M., Stepler, Renne, and Lopez, Mark H. "English Proficiency on the Rise Among Latinos." Pew Research Center. 12 May 2015. Web. 22 May 2015.

Student's Notes:

5/22/15 – by Jens Krogstad, Renne Stepler, Mark Lopez

- *33.2 mill. Hispanics in US speak English well.*
- *2013 – up to 68% from 59% in 2000.*
- *Spanish at home increasing – from 73% to 78%*
- *a record 35.8 million Hispanics speak Spanish at home, a number that has continued to increase as the nation's Hispanic population has grown*

☐ 1 no title of source listed

☐ 2 no author of source listed

☐ 3 inaccurate paraphrase of original text

☐ 4 too many statistics

☐ 5 no quotes around quoted material

☐ 6 no date of access for source listed

Instructors: This is a copy of the Letter to the Editor from pages 170–171 of the Student's Book. The students have already read it in class. You can assign it as a unit writing quiz with the following directions:

1 Read the letter again and annotate it.
2 Write a summary and response. Use your own ideas.

To the Editor:

Last week's article "Success!" by Carol Smith (Op-Ed, June 1) was a well-deserved tribute[1] to this year's graduating seniors. Many of these students belong to "Generation 1.5," a term often used for **immigrants** who moved to the United States from other countries as children or young teens. At the beginning, the author notes the "incredible multiculturalism" of the graduates. However, in the rest of the article, the writer **emphasizes** the benefits of becoming "fully American" and "blending in." This assimilation is a striking contradiction.[2] If we proudly consider ourselves a multicultural society, then why are we so eager for immigrants to adopt American culture at the expense of their native cultures?

The United States has always been a country of immigrants. In fact, only one percent of us are actually Native Americans. The very strength of our nation comes from the rich diversity of ideas, traditions, and languages that people from all over the world have brought. Asking our immigrants to give up their cultures and languages in order to be successful is misguided and damaging.

The message that achieving success requires blending into American culture and shedding[3] one's home culture is not only inconsistent with our history; it is also not **appropriate** as a message for our times. A huge part of our proud history is the waves of immigrants that have come to this country and have shaped our values and traditions. While we hope that immigrants share our values of freedom and individual rights, is it necessary for them to give up their cultures and languages, which bring with them fresh perspectives and innovative ideas? I think not. In addition, in today's global world, being familiar with more than one language and culture is important for development in every area – from education and the arts to science and business. We need other languages and cultures to be competitive in the world.

Furthermore, pressure to become fully integrated into another culture can have a negative effect on people. And I have seen this up close.

[1]**tribute:** something that expresses respect or admiration for someone
[2]**contradiction:** difference between two ideas or facts, both of which cannot be true at the same time
[3]**shed:** get rid of something you do not want

(CONTINUED)

One of my daughter's good friends at school is an immigrant from Thailand. Sarai speaks Thai at home with her parents and English elsewhere. However, she still struggles a bit with the language, especially when she **interacts** with people she doesn't know well. She worries about speaking correctly and fitting in with her American classmates. I wish she could appreciate **the fact that** she is enriching our lives. It's fascinating to listen to her stories about Thailand. I value the opportunity to hear points of view on world events and social issues from someone who isn't "fully American." She helps our family see things from a different perspective and stay open to new ideas. I have told her this many times, but in the outside world, she doesn't get the sense that her difference is valued. Consequently, Sarai feels torn. "It's not fun to be caught between two cultures," she says, "and not really belong to either one."

A friend of mine, Min-jun, immigrated to the United States from Korea. Following his parents' advice, he immersed[4] himself in the new culture and tried to speak only English. He studied hard, did well in school, and graduated with a degree in business. Today he is a respected employee whose fresh ideas help us solve problems in creative ways. Min-jun enjoys his work and is grateful for the opportunities he has had. However, he regrets that much of his native culture has been lost. He can no longer speak Korean well and has difficulty relating to family back home. What a shame (and how unnecessary) that this talented young man was pressured[5] to choose between cultures. He has contributed much to ours, but this has resulted in an unfortunate **shift** in focus away from his own.

According to recent data collected by the U.S. Census Bureau, there are over 40 million immigrants like Sarai and Min-jun in the country today. This is about 13 percent of the total population (or 1 in every 8 people). These people are crucial to our country's development in an increasingly interconnected world. We need to honor and support their biculturalism and send them the right message. As public policy expert Jacob Vigor says, "You can retain[6] a cultural identity and still be an assimilated[7] person." I couldn't agree more. Vigor points the way toward the true road to success, both for our immigrants and our country.

Dr. Carla Banks

Professor of History

Two Peaks College

[4]**immerse:** be completely involved in or part of something
[5]**pressured:** forced to do something
[6]**retain:** keep
[7]**assimilate:** change to become part of a group or society

NAME: ....   DATE: ....

Part A: Academic Vocabulary

Circle the correct words to complete the paragraph.

1   Studies show that multicultural companies with employee **norm / diversity / isolation** often have better communication and more collaboration among employees.

2   Although English is the **motive / norm / diversity** in U.S. businesses, it is important for American employees to be able to communicate with people from all over the world.

3   While some people think that diversity **diminishes / accumulates / evolves** communication, a recent study shows that this is not usually true.

4   Some employers offer training programs to help employees **acknowledge / evolve / accumulate** a variety of skills, such as cross-cultural communication.

5   The desire to learn about different cultures is one **norm / motive / isolation** for moving to another country.

6   Before the Internet was widespread, many remote cultures lived in **motive / diversity / isolation**.

7   Some business owners **acknowledge / diminish / evolve** that there are benefits to hiring skilled workers from different countries.

8   Trumark International Corporation has **acknowledged / accumulated / evolved** since 1995, when it hired its first female director.

Part B: Academic Collocations

Complete the sentences with the academic collocations in the box.

accumulate wealth	cultural diversity	geographical isolation
primary motive	social norms	

1   Many U.S. colleges have more .... than in the 1980s, when most of their students were American.

2   The business's .... for developing a multicultural workplace is to have employees who can communicate with a variety of clients.

3   Children usually learn about their culture's .... from their parents.

4   ...., previously a problem for many countries, is no longer an issue because of Internet access.

5   One way to .... is to invest money in growing industries.

NAME: ....

DATE: ....

Part A

Cross out the extra words to reduce the relative clauses in the sentences.

1 Countries that are showing strong economic growth usually have lower unemployment rates.

2 People who are moving to large cities often find higher salaries but higher housing costs.

3 Companies that are started by entrepreneurs are often successful.

4 Professor Hayman, who is the head of the economics department, teaches Latin American economics.

5 The business-development advisors who were on the board of directors recommended that the company open branches in Europe and Africa.

Part B

Correct the mistake in each sentence.

1 The country small had to seek international investors to help its economy.

2 Communities hoped for economic growth are glad the governor will help them.

3 Tim Simmons, is a cultural-diversity specialist, recommends that international companies hire people from different backgrounds to help their business grow.

4 University courses offering online can connect with students across the globe.

5 The given support by the foreign council allowed Julia Lake to open a store in Thailand.

SCORE: .... / 6

NAME: ....   DATE: ....

Part A

Circle the reasons the students are procrastinating.

1 Mick has to write an essay on female CEOs. He does not know anything about business or business leaders so can't think of anything to write.

   a temptations

   b lack of knowledge

   c distractions

2 Katie's assignment is to write a paper on shifting gender roles in Latin American households. She writes a personal blog about fashion in her free time. Her fans keep emailing with questions. She feels compelled to answer them right away.

   a temptations

   b lack of knowledge

   c distractions

3 Manny is writing an essay on the changing demographics of Los Angeles. He has written some of his paper, but still needs to write a lot more before he's finished. His friend wants him to go out.

   a temptations

   b lack of knowledge

   c distractions

Part B

Match each student from Part A with the most effective strategy for staying focused.

STUDENT	STRATEGY FOR STAYING FOCUSED
☐ 1 Mick	a Don't check email.
☐ 2 Katie	b Have a dedicated study time every day.
☐ 3 Manny	c Ask for help.

Instructors: This is a list of possible prompts to assign as a unit writing quiz.

1 According to a recent National Association of International Educators (NAIE) survey, most Americans think international education is extremely important for future career success. Do you agree or disagree? Provide three reasons and evidence.

2 Some sociologists argue that every society has an underclass, consisting of people who are the poorest and have the least power. Do you think this is true in your culture? Provide reasons and evidence.

3 Studies show that women statistically hold positions that earn less than men's positions. Should companies do more to encourage women to take higher positions that pay more? Why or why not? Provide three reasons and evidence.

4 English has become the language of business. As a result, many people all over the world study English to be more successful in international business. Do you think people should study another language (or languages) besides English to compete in the global economy? Provide three reasons and evidence.

5 Do you think companies should hire people with diverse backgrounds for the sake of diversity even though they might not be the best candidates for the job? Why or why not? Provide three reasons and evidence.

NAME: ....   DATE: ....

Part A: Academic Vocabulary

Circle the correct words to complete the sentences.

1 The recent **access / decline / estimate** of fatal diseases is positive news for poorer countries.

2 Internet **decline / welfare / access** has increased over the last decade, and it is now available almost anywhere in the world.

3 For companies to compete on a global level, they need **comprehensive / estimated / declined** plans to train their employees in the latest technology.

4 Leslie and Trevor Snow volunteer for a global help organization that focuses on improving the **welfare / transformation / access** of the world's poor children.

5 Building affordable homes and health centers has caused a **decline / transformation / welfare** in formerly poor neighborhoods.

6 According to an **estimate / issue / access** by the Pew Research Center, U.S. population growth will decrease between now and 2050.

7 The charities on this website are trying to solve global **transformations / declines / issues** such as overpopulation, hunger, and limited health care.

8 A local non-profit group is **declining / implementing / estimating** a plan to help refugees.

Part B: Academic Phrases

Complete the paragraph with the correct form of academic phrases in the box.

in the absence of	on the basis of	with respect to

.... good local health care, some poorer nations cannot manage the spread of
                        (1)
diseases without the help of other nations. Therefore, the World Health Institute is now offering training

courses in global health studies. Students will be accepted into the courses ....
                                                                              (2)
their undergraduate grades in science and math. Once the students finish the courses, the Institute will send

them to volunteer at health centers throughout the world. .... the future, the Institute
                                                              (3)
is confident that graduates of the program will find employment in the global communities that need the

most help.

NAME: ....

DATE: ....

Part A

Choose the correct modals to complete the sentences.

1 College graduates who want to help those less fortunate **can / must** join the Peace Corps.

2 To help unemployed adults learn a new skill, community colleges **may / should** offer free classes.

3 The government **could / will** support single parents by creating a program to provide such services as house cleaning and babysitting.

4 If the company doesn't offer better salaries and benefits, the employees **should / will** quit.

5 While it **should / may** be true that international aid funds help with natural disasters, a lot of help comes from private citizens.

6 The organization **must / might** be more successful if it recruits more volunteers.

Part B

Correct the mistake in each sentence.

1 Students interested in helping with the book-collection project should seeing Professor Tripp after class.

2 If the agency will require a passport for identification, Jorge won't be able to work there.

3 The author's argument might be not valid because the research shows that globalization actually

helps countries.

NAME: ....   DATE: ....

Read the student writer's synthesis. Then match the numbers of the sentences from the synthesis with the student's purposes.

(1) California provides the majority of the produce from broccoli to tree nuts to the United States, but the state and the nation's produce are in trouble because of the historic drought. (2) Two scholars, Drs. Kevin Whitman and Trudy Connors, have suggested alternative ways to grow food during these times of drought. (3–4) Dr. Whitman, an agriculturalist at the non-profit group Save the Green, suggests we build massive greenhouses in states not prone to drought such as Florida and Maine. He predicts most low-lying food such as lettuces, broccoli, peppers, and carrots will be able to grow in quantities almost as large as the current crop in California. (5) Dr. Connors of California University suggests desalinating ocean water for irrigation purposes. (6) She disagrees with Whitman, suggesting that if California produce were to grow elsewhere, it would severely hurt California's economy. (7) Both scholars, however, do agree that the drought will force us to think of immediate solutions. (8) Their plans make sense because if the very dry climate in California continues, there will most certainly be a need for a different way to grow food.

SENTENCE(S)	PURPOSE
☐ 1	a Cite names of experts that student writer included
☐ 2	b Cite the first expert's opinion
☐ 3–4	c Cite the second expert's opinion
☐ 5	d Draw conclusions about the experts' ideas
☐ 6	e Note the differences between two authors' ideas
☐ 7	f Note the similarities between two authors' ideas
☐ 8	g State student writer's opinion

Instructors: This is a list of possible prompts to assign as a unit writing quiz.

1 With increased globalization, some nations are adopting the language and culture of other nations.
Is this a positive or negative thing? Provide reasons and evidence. Include at least one counterargument and refutation. Explain.

2 Do you think learning a second language should be required for all high-school students? Why or why not? Provide reasons and evidence. Include at least one counterargument and refutation.

3 Some students travel abroad after high school before starting college. Do you think this is a good idea? Provide reasons and evidence. Include at least one counterargument and refutation.

4 When a natural disaster such as a volcano or earthquake occurs in a poorer nation, is it the responsibility of wealthier nations to help? Provide reasons and evidence. Include at least one counterargument and refutation.

5 Many international aid organizations that help developing countries, such as Doctors Without Borders, are financed by individual donors. Do you think governments should financially support such international organizations? Provide reasons and evidence. Include at least one counterargument and refutation.

UNIT QUIZZES ANSWER KEY

UNIT 1

Unit 1 Vocabulary

Part A

1 community
2 cooperation
3 supply
4 sufficient
5 transition
6 source
7 scope
8 basis

Part B

1 water supply
2 sense of community
3 limited supply
4 on a daily basis
5 wide scope

Unit 1 Grammar

Part A

1 to convert
2 to preserve
3 to call
4 to recycle
5 to waste
6 to volunteer

Part B

1 The Environmental Studies professors discussed *holding* ~~to hold~~ classes in a local city park so students would get a first-hand view of the local environment.

2 When gas prices decrease, people tend to *not* ~~not~~ buy hybrid cars.

3 Many grocery stores no longer provide plastic bags *to* ~~for~~ help save the environment.

Unit 1 Avoiding Plagiarism

Part A

Circle: 2 (Student Text B)

Part B

1 **Student Text A:** Air quality in Beijing and several other major cities reached record lows, and the public is increasingly taking note of this issue. In an increase of 11 percentage points from 2012, nearly half (47%) rate air pollution a very big problem. Forty percent say water pollution is also a concern, after thousands of dead pigs floating down a river through the center of Shanghai.

2 **Student Text B:** Air and water pollution are concerns in China. In January 2013, air quality in major Chinese cities reached record lows. Forty-seven percent think air pollution is a very big problem, which is up 11% from 2012. And following a year that included headlines about thousands of dead pigs floating down a river through the center of Shanghai, concerns about water pollution have also increased. Four-in-ten say it is a very big problem, compared with 33% in 2012.

UNIT 2

Unit 2 Vocabulary

Part A

1 fundamental
2 assume
3 rely on
4 expectations
5 task
6 factor
7 gap
8 persistence

Part B

1 c   2 a   3 b

Unit 2 Grammar

Part A

1 Teachers typically believe *that* students learn better when they are interested in the material.

2 The researchers concluded *that* most children who read extensively at home become better writers.

3 Education experts argue *that* studying multiple disciplines such as math, science, languages, and the arts, results in more well-balanced students.

4 The claim *that* standardized testing, such as the ACT or SAT, does not measure academic ability is debatable.

Part B

1 Many parents think that children *are* spending too much time on computers in school these days.

2 Maria told her education professor that *she* would write her paper on learning technology.

3 Studies show experiential learning (i.e., learning by doing) *that* can benefit many students.

Unit 2 Avoiding Plagiarism

Paraphrase 1: b
Paraphrase 2: c
Paraphrase 3: a

UNIT 3

Unit 3 Vocabulary

Part A

1	survive	5	identical
2	impact	6	participate
3	network	7	adapt
4	infrastructure	8	framework

Part B

1	had an impact	4	nearly identical
2	Social networks	5	social impact
3	An extensive network		

Unit 3 Grammar

Part A

1 Neighborhoods (that) hold monthly parties or events have a strong sense of community.
2 The doctor (who) volunteers at the clinic likes to help the needy.
3 The School Supply Bank collects school supplies for parents (who) do not have enough money to buy them for their children.
4 The city leader (whom) Mrs. Delfano called promised to help her organization raise money.
5 Children (whose) parents show self-discipline typically have a strong work ethic in school.
6 Sibling relationships (that) are strong in childhood often remain strong in adulthood.

Part B

1	who	4	who
2	where	5	who
3	whom	6	which

Unit 3 Avoiding Plagiarism

Part A

Check: 1, 3, 4

Part B

Check: 2, 3, 5

UNIT 4

Unit 4 Vocabulary

Part A

1	generations	5	promote
2	perspective	6	scenario
3	enables	7	ongoing
4	aware	8	inherent

Part B

1 One effect of
2 Another impact of
3 as a result of

Unit 4 Grammar

Part A

1	post, will not hire	5	is, do not have
2	are, contribute	6	will receive, join
3	publishes, post	7	share, get
4	will attract, shares	8	have, will find

Part B

1 If children ~~will~~ use social-media too much, they might post pictures of themselves they might later regret.

2 Restaurant and hotel owners can attract more customers if they ~~uploads~~ upload videos of successful events on social-media sites.

3 If students want to respond privately to a professor's message to the entire class, they should not hit the "reply all" button.

4 When students take online classes, they will be able to take the class anywhere and ~~when they take online classes they will~~ meet people from all over the world.

5 Posting photos and updates on social-media sites is a good way to keep in touch, if your family and friends live far away.

Unit 4 Avoiding Plagiarism

Part A

1	a, c	2	a	3	a, b, d

Part B

1	b	2	a	3	b

Unit 5 Vocabulary

Part A

1. a global
2. experiments
3. focus
4. conscious
5. ensure
6. urge
7. sense
8. consumes

Part B

1. The main focus of
2. made a conscious decision
3. a strong urge
4. conducted an experiment
5. makes sense

Unit 5 Grammar

Part A

1. shows
2. concluded
3. presented
4. argues
5. found
6. gave

Part B

(1) Most research ~~says~~ *demonstrates / shows / finds that* the majority of workers seem content in their jobs. (2) However, Landry, in his independent study on work satisfaction, found *that* ^ only 46% of the people whom he interviewed were happy with their jobs. (3) Participants in Landry's study described ~~that~~ difficulties in trying to find satisfaction in their current jobs. (4) Landry concluded *that* ^ while his study was small, the results were significant enough to give reason for further research.

Unit 5 Avoiding Plagiarism

Part A

1. b   2. c   3. d   4. a

Part B

Check: 1, 2, 4

Unit 6 Vocabulary

Part A

1. instance
2. shift
3. emphasize
4. appropriate
5. ignore
6. various
7. immigrants
8. interact

Part B

1. The fact that
2. in part
3. For this reason

Unit 6 Grammar

Part A

1. are offered
2. are given
3. is required
4. were invited
5. was encouraged
6. was chosen

Part B

1. Last Monday, Professor Harte's students ~~was~~ *were* tested on relative clauses.
2. Arabic and Japanese are ~~been~~ *being* taught in Sydney public schools.
3. François was glad that the spelling rules ~~was~~ *were* posted on the wall of his classroom.
4. The cross-cultural curriculum ~~was~~ helped students understand different cultures.
5. The bilingual curriculum is ~~been~~ *being* adopted by most of the schools in the area.

Unit 6 Avoiding Plagiarism

Part A

1. source
2. understanding
3. notes
4. code
5. Organize

Part B

Check: 1, 3, 5

UNIT 7

Unit 7 Vocabulary

Part A

1 diversity
2 norm
3 diminishes
4 accumulate

5 motive
6 isolation
7 acknowledge
8 evolved

Part B

1 cultural diversity
2 primary motive
3 social norms

4 Geographical isolation
5 accumulate wealth

Unit 7 Grammar

Part A

1 Countries ~~that are~~ showing strong economic growth usually have lower unemployment rates.
2 People ~~who are~~ moving to large cities often find higher salaries but higher housing costs.
3 Companies ~~that were~~ started by entrepreneurs are often successful.
4 Professor Hayman, ~~who is~~ the head of the economics department, teaches Latin American economics.
5 The business-development advisors ~~who were~~ on the board of directors recommended that the company open branches in Europe and Africa.

Part B

1 The ~~country small~~ _small country_ had to seek international investors to help its economy.
2 Communities ~~hoped~~ _hoping_ for economic growth are glad the governor will help them.
3 Tim Simmons, ~~is~~ a cultural-diversity specialist, recommends that international companies hire people from different backgrounds to help their business grow.
4 University courses ~~offering~~ _offered_ online can connect with students across the globe.
5 The ~~given support~~ _support given_ by the foreign council allowed Julia Lake to open a store in Thailand.

Unit 7 Avoiding Plagiarism

Part A

1 b   2 c   3 a

Part B

1 c   2 a   3 b

UNIT 8

Unit 8 Vocabulary

Part A

1 decline
2 access
3 comprehensive
4 welfare

5 transformation
6 estimate
7 issues
8 implementing

Part B

1 In the absence of
2 on the basis of
3 With respect to

Unit 8 Grammar

Part A

1 can
2 should
3 could

4 will
5 may
6 might

Part B

1 Students interested in helping with the book-collection project should ~~seeing~~ _see_ Professor Tripp after class.
2 If the agency ~~will require~~ _requires_ a passport for identification, Jorge won't be able to work there.
3 The author's argument might ~~be not~~ _not be_ valid because the research shows that globalization actually helps countries.

Unit 8 Avoiding Plagiarism

Sentence 1: g
Sentence 2: a
Sentences 3–4: b
Sentence 5: c

Sentence 6: e
Sentence 7: f
Sentence 8: d

UNIT QUIZZES WRITING RUBRIC

Final Draft Writing Assignment Rubric

CATEGORY	CRITERIA	SCORE
Language Use	Grammar and vocabulary are accurate, appropriate, and varied. Sentence types are varied and used appropriately. Level of formality (register) shows a good understanding of audience and purpose. Mechanics (capitalization, punctuation, indentation, and spelling) are strong.	
Organization & Mode (structure)	Writing is well organized and follows the conventions of academic writing: • Paragraph – topic sentence, supporting details, concluding sentence • Essay – introduction with thesis, body paragraphs, conclusion Rhetorical mode is used correctly and appropriately. Research is clearly and correctly integrated into student writing (if applicable).	
Coherence, Clarity, & Unity	Sentences within a paragraph flow logically with appropriate transitions; paragraphs within an essay flow logically with appropriate transitions. Sentences and ideas are clear and make sense to the reader. All sentences in a paragraph relate to the topic sentence; all paragraphs in an essay relate to the thesis.	
Content & Development (meaning)	Writing completes the task and fully answers the prompt. Content is meaningful and interesting. Main points and ideas are fully developed with good support and logic.	

How well does the response meet the criteria?	Recommended Score
At least 90%	25
At least 80%	20
At least 70%	15
At least 60%	10
At least 50%	5
Less than 50%	0
Total Score Possible per Section	25
Total Score Possible	100

Feedback:

NOTES